Coaching Youth Volleyball

FOURTH EDITION

FOUNT[...]DALE PUBLIC LIBRARY DISTRICT
[3]00 West Briarcliff Road
[Bo]lingbrook, IL 60440-2894
(630) 759-21[0]2

American Sport Education Program

Recommended by USA Volleyball

Human Kinetics

Library of Congress Cataloging-in-Publication Data

Coaching youth volleyball / American Sport Education Program. -- 4th ed.
    p. cm.
"Recommended by USA Volleyball."
ISBN-13: 978-0-7360-6820-8 (soft cover)
ISBN-10: 0-7360-6820-1 (soft cover)
1. Volleyball for children--Coaching. 2. Volleyball--Coaching. I. American Sport Education Program.
GV1015.5.C63 2007
796.325--dc22

                         2007006277

ISBN-10: 0-7360-6820-1
ISBN-13: 978-0-7360-6820-8

Copyright © 2007, 2001, 1997, 1993 by Human Kinetics, Inc.

All rights reserved. Except for use in a review, the reproduction or utilization of this work in any form or by any electronic, mechanical, or other means, now known or hereafter invented, including xerography, photocopying, and recording, and in any information storage and retrieval system, is forbidden without the written permission of the publisher.

Notice: Permission to reproduce the following material is granted to instructors and agencies who have purchased *Coaching Youth Volleyball, Fourth Edition*: pp. 166-171. The reproduction of other parts of this book is expressly forbidden by the above copyright notice. Persons or agencies who have not purchased *Coaching Youth Volleyball, Fourth Edition*, may not reproduce any material.

The Web addresses cited in this text were current as of April 2007, unless otherwise noted.

Acquisitions Editor: Amy Tocco; **Project Writers:** Diana Cole and John Kessel; **Developmental Editor:** Laura Floch; **Assistant Editor:** Cory Weber; **Copyeditor:** Pat Connolly; **Proofreader:** Bethany Bentley; **Permission Manager:** Carly Breeding; **Graphic Designer:** Nancy Rasmus; **Graphic Artist:** Tara Welsch; **Cover Designer:** Keith Blomberg; **Photographer (cover):** Jim Huffman; **Photographer (interior):** Tim De Frisco; photos on pages 1, 11, 21, 43, 57, 61, 67, 81, 111, 135, and 149 © Jim Huffman; **Photo Asset Manager:** Laura Fitch; **Visual Production Assistant:** Joyce Brumfield; **Photo Office Assistant:** Jason Allen; **Art Manager:** Kelly Hendren; **Illustrator:** Al Wilborn; **Printer:** United Graphics

We thank Colorado College in Colorado Springs, CO for assistance in providing the location for the photo shoot for this book.

Copies of this book are available at special discounts for bulk purchase for sales promotions, premiums, fund-raising, or educational use. Special editions or book excerpts can also be created to specifications. For details, contact the Special Sales Manager at Human Kinetics.

Printed in the United States of America   10 9 8 7 6 5 4 3 2

Human Kinetics
Web site: www.HumanKinetics.com

United States: Human Kinetics
P.O. Box 5076
Champaign, IL 61825-5076
800-747-4457
e-mail: humank@hkusa.com

Canada: Human Kinetics   .
475 Devonshire Road, Unit 100
Windsor, ON N8Y 2L5
800-465-7301 (in Canada only)
e-mail: info@hkcanada.com

Europe: Human Kinetics
107 Bradford Road
Stanningley
Leeds LS28 6AT, United Kingdom
+44 (0)113 255 5665
e-mail: hk@hkeurope.com

Australia: Human Kinetics
57A Price Avenue
Lower Mitcham, South Australia 5062
08 8372 0999
e-mail: info@hkaustralia.com

New Zealand: Human Kinetics
Division of Sports Distributors NZ Ltd.
P.O. Box 300 226 Albany
North Shore City, Auckland
0064 9 448 1207
e-mail: info@humankinetics.co.nz

Contents

Welcome to Coaching

Coaching young people is an exciting way to be involved in sport. But it isn't easy. Some coaches are overwhelmed by the responsibilities involved in helping athletes through their early sport experiences. And that's not surprising, because coaching youngsters requires more than bringing the balls to the court and letting them play. It involves preparing them physically and mentally to compete effectively, fairly, and safely in their sport and providing them with a positive role model.

This book will help you meet the challenges and experience the many rewards of coaching young athletes. In this book you'll learn how to meet your responsibilities as a coach, communicate well, provide for safety, and teach skills in a fun way. You'll also learn strategies for coaching on game day. To help you with your practices, 18 drills are included throughout the text and in appendix C. We also provide sample practice plans and season plans to guide you through your season.

USA Volleyball's Coaching Accreditation Program (CAP) accepts ASEP's Coaching Youth Volleyball online course, for which this book serves as the text, as a CAP module toward certification. If you would like more information about USA Volleyball's Coaching Accreditation Program (CAP), contact USAV at cap@usav.org or 719-228-6800. For more information on other American Sport Education Program courses and resources, please contact us at the following address:

ASEP
P.O. Box 5076
Champaign, IL 61825-5076
800-747-5698
www.ASEP.com

Welcome From USA Volleyball

On behalf of USA Volleyball, welcome to *Coaching Youth Volleyball*. It is one of many resources available to you through the American Sport Education Program (ASEP) and USA Volleyball. Whether you're learning how to teach proper fundamental skills, how to create efficient drills and practices, or how to communicate better, this book can guide you through your experience.

You will find this book easy to follow and an excellent introduction to youth coaching with fresh ideas on how to coach children in the sport of volleyball. These methods may be very different from the way you were coached, but they are best for developing and mentoring passionate players who can, in turn, pass their knowledge on to younger kids and help expose them to the game. This book contains information on how to coach a successful team starting with the first day of practice to the final game of the season, while along the way teaching young players valuable skills. Also included are fun activities and plenty of resources to aid you in your coaching journey. These coaching methods are based on our experiences in teaching the many youth and junior USA Volleyball coaches across the country, from the IMPACT Level up through the Coaching Accreditation Program (CAP) Level I, II, and III courses.

USA Volleyball's educational mission is to encourage and educate coaches about their tremendous opportunities and responsibilities for influencing today's youth. In working with the American Sport Education Program (ASEP), our goal is to provide youth coaches with effective resources to help expand their knowledge of the sport and ensure that every coach and every player has a positive experience. For you, the benefits of coaching last a lifetime; your coaching will have a profound effect on the many players you influence—not just for today, but for many years to come. Thank you for coaching youth volleyball!

Sincerely,

Diana L. Cole
USA Volleyball
Director of Coaching Education Programs and USAV-CAP Cadre member

John Kessel
USA Volleyball
Director of Membership Development and Disabled Programs and USAV-CAP Cadre Member, FIVB International Instructor, and Master IMPACT Instructor

Drill Finder

Key to Diagrams

(B) Blocker

(CB) Center-back player

(CF) Center-front player

(H) Hitter

(LB) Left-back player

(LF) Left-front player

(P) Passer

(RB) Right-back player

(RF) Right-front player

(Sv) Server

(S) Setter

(Ts) Tosser

◯ Player, when position is not applicable

————————→ Path of player

— — — — — → Path of ball

1

Stepping Into Coaching

I f you are like most youth league coaches today, you have probably been recruited from the ranks of concerned parents, sport enthusiasts, or community volunteers. Like many rookie and veteran coaches, you probably have had little formal instruction on how to coach. But when the call went out for coaches to assist with the local youth volleyball program, you answered because you like children and enjoy volleyball, and perhaps because you wanted to be involved in a worthwhile community activity.

Your initial coaching assignment may be difficult. Like many volunteers, you may not know everything there is to know about volleyball or about how to work with children. *Coaching Youth Volleyball* presents the basics of coaching volleyball effectively. To start, we look at your responsibilities and what's involved in being a coach. We also talk about what to do when your own child is on the team you coach, and we examine five tools for being an effective coach.

Your Responsibilities as a Coach

Coaching at any level involves much more than creating a service order or teaching your players how to execute a pass, set, attack sequence. Coaching involves accepting the tremendous responsibility you face when parents put their children into your care. As a volleyball coach, you'll be called on to do the following:

1. *Provide a safe physical environment.*

   Playing volleyball involves some inherent risks, which will be discussed more in chapter 4, but as a coach you're responsible for regularly inspecting the courts and equipment used for practice and competition (see "Facilities and Equipment Checklist" in appendix A on page 166). You should reassure players and parents that you will be teaching the safest techniques in order to help players avoid injury and that you have an emergency action plan in place (see chapter 4 for more information).

2. *Communicate in a positive way.*

   As you can already see, you have a lot to communicate. You'll communicate not only with your players and their parents, but also with the coaching staff, officials, administrators, and others. Communicate in a way that is positive and that demonstrates that you have the best interests of the players at heart (see chapter 2 for more information).

3. *Teach the fundamental skills of volleyball.*

   When teaching the fundamental skills of volleyball, keep in mind that volleyball is a game, and therefore, you want to be sure that your players have fun. We ask that you help all players be the best they can be by creating a fun, yet productive, practice environment. To help you do this, we'll show you an innovative games approach to teaching and practicing the skills young players need to know—an approach that kids thoroughly enjoy (see chapter 5 for more information). Additionally, to help your players improve their skills, you need to have a sound understanding of offensive and defensive skills. We'll provide information to assist you in gaining that understanding (see chapters 7 and 8 for more information).

4. *Teach the rules of volleyball.*

You need to introduce the rules of volleyball and incorporate them into individual instruction (see chapter 3 for more information). Many rules can be taught during practice, including rules related to contacting the ball, determining whether a ball is in bounds or out of bounds, net violations, and service and service rotation (overlap) rules. You should plan to review the rules any time an opportunity naturally arises in practices.

5. *Direct players in competition.*

Your responsibilities include determining starting lineups and a substitution plan, relating appropriately to officials and to opposing coaches and players, and making sound tactical decisions during games (see chapter 9 for more information on coaching during games). Remember that the focus is not on winning at all costs, but on coaching your kids to compete well, do their best, improve their volleyball skills, strive to win within the rules—and most of all, have fun!

6. *Help your players become fit and value fitness for a lifetime.*

We want you to help your players be fit so they can play volleyball safely and successfully. We also want your players to learn to become fit on their own, understand the value of fitness, and enjoy training. Thus, we ask you not to make them do push-ups or run laps for punishment. Make it fun to get fit for volleyball, and make it fun to play volleyball so that they'll stay fit for a lifetime.

7. *Help young people develop character.*

Character development includes learning, caring, being honest and respectful, and taking responsibility. These intangible qualities are no less important to teach than the skill of hitting the volleyball. We ask you to teach these values to players by demonstrating and encouraging behaviors that express these values at all times. For example, in teaching good team defense, stress to young players the importance of playing within the rules, showing respect for their opponents, and learning to back each other up, even when they aren't directly involved in passing the ball or attacking a set.

These are your responsibilities as a coach. Remember that every player is an individual. You must provide a wholesome environment in which every player has the opportunity to learn how to play the game without fear while having fun and enjoying the overall volleyball experience.

Coaching Your Own Child

Coaching can become even more complicated when your child plays on the team you coach. Many coaches are parents, but the two roles should not be confused. As a parent, you are responsible only for yourself and your child, but as a coach you are also responsible for the organization, all the players on the team, and their parents. Because of this additional responsibility, your behavior on the volleyball court will be different from your behavior at home, and your child may not understand why.

For example, imagine the confusion of a young girl who is the center of her parents' attention at home but is barely noticed by her father (who is the coach) in the sport setting. Or consider the mixed signals received by a young player whose skill is constantly evaluated by a coach (who is also her mother) who otherwise rarely comments on her daughter's activities. You need to explain to your child your new responsibilities and how they will affect your relationship when coaching. Take the following steps to avoid problems in coaching your own child:

- Ask your child if she wants you to coach the team.
- Explain why you want to be involved with the team.
- Discuss with your child how your interactions will change when you take on the role of coach at practices or games.
- Limit your coaching behavior to when you are in the coaching role.
- Avoid parenting during practice or game situations to keep your role clear in your child's mind.
- Reaffirm your love for your child, irrespective of her performance on the volleyball court.

Coaching Tip

Be sure to discuss your interest in coaching the volleyball team with your child before making a decision. If your child has strong reservations about you taking the job of head coach, you should consider becoming involved in a smaller role instead. For example, you can be an assistant coach, serve as the scorekeeper or announcer for the team, or organize a group of parents who provide drinks and snacks at practices and games.

Five Tools of an Effective Coach

Have you purchased the traditional coaching tools—things such as whistles, coaching clothes, sport shoes, and a clipboard? They'll help you in the act of coaching, but to be successful, you'll need five other tools that cannot be bought. These tools are available only through self-examination and hard work; they're easy to remember with the acronym COACH:

C   Comprehension

O   Outlook

A   Affection

C   Character

H   Humor

Comprehension

Comprehension of the rules and skills of volleyball is required. You must understand the basic elements of the sport. To improve your comprehension of volleyball, take the following steps:

- Read about the rules of volleyball in chapter 3 of this book.
- Read about the fundamental skills of volleyball in chapters 7 and 8.
- Read additional volleyball coaching books, including those available from the American Sport Education Program (ASEP).
- Contact youth volleyball organizations, such as USA Volleyball (USAV) or the United States Youth Volleyball League (USYVL).
- Attend volleyball coaching clinics, such as those offered by USA Volleyball's Coaching Accreditation Program (CAP).
- Talk with more experienced coaches.
- Observe local college, high school, youth, and USAV Junior Club volleyball games.
- Watch volleyball games on television.
- Watch instructional DVDs and videotapes on volleyball, such as those offered by USA Volleyball's Coaching Accreditation Program or the American Volleyball Coaches Association.

In addition to having volleyball knowledge, you must implement proper training and safety methods so that your players can participate with little risk of injury. Even then, injuries may occur. And more often than not, you'll be the first person responding to your players' injuries, so be sure you understand the basic emergency care procedures described in chapter 4. Also, read in that chapter how to handle more serious sport injury situations.

Coaching Tip
Attending local college, high school, or USAV Junior Club games is a low-cost way not only for you to improve your knowledge of the game, but also for players of all ages to observe the technical and tactical skills of volleyball. Consider working with your players' parents to organize a team outing to a local game in place of an after-school or weekend practice.

Outlook

This coaching tool refers to your perspective and goals—what you seek as a coach. The most common coaching objectives are to (a) have fun; (b) help players develop their physical, mental, and social skills; and (c) strive to win. Thus, your outlook involves your priorities, your planning, and your vision for the future. See "Assessing Your Priorities" to learn more about the priorities you set for yourself as a coach.

ASEP has a motto that will help you keep your outlook in line with the best interests of the kids on your team. It summarizes in four words all you need to remember when establishing your coaching priorities:

Athletes First, Winning Second

This motto recognizes that striving to win is an important, even vital, part of sports. But it emphatically states that no efforts in striving to win should be made at the expense of the athletes' well-being, development, and enjoyment. Take the following actions to better define your outlook:

- With the members of your coaching staff, determine your priorities for the season.
- Prepare for situations that may challenge your priorities.
- Set goals for yourself and your players that are consistent with your priorities.
- Plan how you and your players can best attain your goals.
- Review your goals frequently to be sure that you are staying on track.

Affection

Another vital tool you will want to have in your coaching kit is a genuine concern for the young people you coach. This requires having an enthusiasm for working with kids, a desire to share with them your enjoyment and knowledge of volleyball, and the patience and understanding that allow all your players to grow from their involvement in sport. You can demonstrate your affection and patience in many ways, including the following:

- Make an effort to get to know each player on your team, as well as what motivates each player to be there.
- Treat each player as an individual.
- Empathize with players trying to learn new and difficult skills.
- Treat players as you would like to be treated under similar circumstances.
- Control your emotions.
- Show your enthusiasm for being involved with your team.
- Keep an upbeat tempo and positive tone in all of your communications.

Assessing Your Priorities

Even though all coaches focus on competition, we want you to focus on *positive* competition—keeping the pursuit of victory in perspective by making decisions that, first, are in the best interest of the players, and second, will help to win the game.

So, how do you know if your outlook and priorities are in order? Here's a little test:

1. Which situation would you be most proud of?
   a. *knowing that each participant enjoyed playing volleyball*
   b. *seeing that all players improved their volleyball skills*
   c. *winning the league championship*

2. Which statement best reflects your thoughts about sport?
   a. *If it isn't fun, don't do it.*
   b. *Everyone should learn something every day.*
   c. *Sport isn't fun if you don't win.*

3. How would you like your players to remember you?
   a. *as a coach who was fun to play for*
   b. *as a coach who provided a good base of fundamental skills*
   c. *as a coach who had a winning record*

4. Which would you most like to hear a parent of a player on your team say?
   a. *Amy really had a good time playing volleyball this year.*
   b. *Nicole learned some important lessons playing volleyball this year.*
   c. *Josh played on the first-place volleyball team this year.*

5. Which of the following would be the most rewarding moment of your season?
   a. *having your team want to continue playing, even after practice is over*
   b. *seeing one of your players finally master the skill of forearm passing*
   c. *winning the league championship*

Look over your answers. If you most often selected "a" responses, then having fun is most important to you. A majority of "b" answers suggests that skill development is what attracts you to coaching. And if "c" was your most frequent response, winning is tops on your list of coaching priorities. If your priorities are in order, your players' well-being will take precedence over your team's win–loss record every time.

Character

The fact that you have decided to coach young volleyball players probably means that you think participation in sport is important. But whether or not that participation develops character in your players depends as much on you as it does on the sport itself. How can you help your players build character?

To teach kids good character, coaches must model appropriate behaviors for sport and life. That means more than just saying the right things. What you say and what you do must match. There is no place in coaching for the "Do as I say, not as I do" philosophy. Challenge, support, encourage, and reward every youngster, and your players will be more likely to accept, even celebrate, their differences. Be in control before, during, and after all practices and games. And don't be afraid to admit that you were wrong. No one is perfect!

Each member of your coaching staff should consider the following steps to becoming a good role model:

- Always behave ethically and make ethical decisions regarding your team, your players, and your own life.
- Take stock of your strengths and weaknesses.
- Build on your strengths.
- Set goals for yourself to improve on those areas that you don't want to see copied by your players.
- If you slip up, apologize to your team and to yourself. You'll do better next time.

Coaching Tip

It has been shown that kids need opportunities to demonstrate competence, influence, and affiliation. To allow your players to demonstrate competence, you can give each player an opportunity to show other players something that she can do well, even if it isn't volleyball specific. For influence, you can let players (depending on the age level) have input on team rules, policies, goals, and so on. And for affiliation, you can allow players to express that they are part of a unique group by wearing team T-shirts outside of practice or games, hair ribbons of a certain color, and so forth.

Humor

Humor is an often-overlooked coaching tool—however, please keep in mind that sarcasm is never a way to inject humor when coaching kids. For our use, humor means having the ability to laugh at yourself and with your players during practices and games. Nothing helps balance the seriousness of a practice session as effectively as the team and coaches enjoying a chuckle or two. And a sense of humor puts in perspective the many mistakes your players will make. So don't get upset over each miscue or respond negatively to erring players. Allow your players and yourself to enjoy the ups, and don't dwell on the downs. Here are some tips for injecting humor and fun into your practices:

- Make practices fun by including a variety of activities.
- Keep all players involved in games and skill practices.
- Consider laughter by your players to be a sign of enjoyment, not of waning discipline.
- Smile!

2

Communicating
As a Coach

I n chapter 1, you learned about the tools you need for coaching: comprehension, outlook, affection, character, and humor. These are essentials for effective coaching; without them, you'd have a difficult time getting started. But none of the tools will work if you don't know how to use them with your players—and this requires skillful communication. This chapter examines what communication is and how you can become a more effective communicator.

Coaches often mistakenly believe that communication occurs only when instructing players to do something, but verbal commands are only a small part of the communication process. More than half of what is communicated is done so nonverbally. So remember when you are coaching: Actions speak louder than words.

Communication in its simplest form involves two people: a sender and a receiver. The sender transmits the message verbally, through facial expressions, and possibly through body language. Once the message is sent, the receiver must receive it and, optimally, understand it. A receiver who fails to pay attention or listen will miss part, if not all, of the message.

Sending Effective Messages

Young players often have little understanding of the rules and skills of volleyball and probably even less confidence in their ability to play the game. So they need accurate, understandable, and supportive messages to help them along. That's why your verbal and nonverbal messages are important.

Verbal Messages

"Sticks and stones may break my bones, but words will never hurt me" isn't true. Spoken words can have a strong and long-lasting effect. And coaches' words are particularly influential because youngsters place great importance on what coaches say. Perhaps you, like many former youth sport participants, have a difficult time remembering much of anything you were told by your elementary school teachers, but you can probably still recall several specific things your coaches at that level said to you. Such is the lasting effect of a coach's comments to a player.

Whether you are correcting misbehavior, teaching a player how to hit the ball, or praising a player for good effort, you should consider a number of things when sending a message verbally:

- Be positive and honest.
- State it clearly and simply.
- Say it loud enough, and say it again.
- Be consistent.

Be Positive and Honest

Nothing turns people off like hearing someone nag all the time, and players react similarly to a coach who gripes constantly or who critiques every contact and move a player makes. Kids particularly need encouragement because they often doubt their ability to perform in a sport. So look for and tell your players what they did well. In other words, catch them doing it right!

But don't cover up poor or incorrect play with rosy words of praise. Kids know all too well when they've erred, and no cheerfully expressed cliche can undo their mistakes. If you fail to acknowledge players' errors, your players will think you are a phony.

An effective way to correct a performance error is to first point out the part of the skill that the player performed correctly. Then explain—in a positive manner—the error that the player made and show her the correct way to do it. Finish by encouraging the player and emphasizing the correct performance. An example might be, "Josh, I like the way you kept your elbow up on your arm swing that time. Next time I want you to swing your arm as fast as you can, and remember to keep that elbow up!"

Be sure not to follow a positive statement with the word *but*. A better technique is to substitute the word *and* whenever you feel you might say *but*. For example, you shouldn't say, "That was a good approach on your attack, Kelly, but you didn't contact the ball at the peak of your jump." This causes many kids to ignore the positive statement and focus on the negative one. Instead, you could say, "That was a good approach on your attack, Kelly. And if you contact the ball at the peak of your jump, you'll be able to get more zip on the ball and get a better angle on your spike. Way to go."

State It Clearly and Simply

Positive and honest messages are good, but only if expressed directly in words your players understand. Beating around the bush is ineffective and inefficient. And if you ramble, your players will miss the point of your message and probably lose interest. Here are some tips for saying things clearly:

- Organize your thoughts before speaking to your players.
- Know your subject as completely as possible.
- Be specific with feedback and give it immediately following the situation.
- Explain things thoroughly, but don't bore your players with long-winded monologues.
- Use language your players can understand, and be consistent in your terminology. However, avoid trying to be hip by using their age group's slang.

Say It Loud Enough, and Say It Again

Talk to your team in a voice that all members can hear. A crisp, vigorous voice commands attention and respect; garbled and weak speech is tuned out. It's okay and, in fact, appropriate to soften your voice when speaking to a player individually about a personal problem. But most of the time your messages will be for all your players to hear, so make sure they can! An enthusiastic voice also motivates players and tells them you enjoy being their coach. A word of caution, however: Avoid dominating the setting with a booming voice that distracts attention from players' performances.

Sometimes what you say, even if stated loudly and clearly, won't sink in the first time. This may be particularly true when young players hear words they don't understand. To avoid boring repetition and still get your message across, you can say the same thing in a slightly different way. For instance, you might first tell your players, "When you're passing, remember to keep a flat surface with your forearms!" If they don't appear to understand, you might say, "When your forearms are flat, you can direct the pass better. Otherwise the ball could bounce off in just about any direction." The second form of the message may get through to players who missed it the first time around.

> **Coaching Tip**
>
> Remember, terms that you are familiar with and understand may be completely foreign to your players, especially younger players or beginners. Adjust your vocabulary to match the age group. Although 12- to 14-year-olds may understand terms such as "better the ball" or "serve the seams," 8- and 9-year-olds may be confused by this terminology. In some cases, you may need to use demonstrations with the players so they can "see" the term and how it relates to the game of volleyball.

Be Consistent

People often say things in ways that imply a different message. For example, a touch of sarcasm added to the words "Way to go!" sends an entirely different message than the words themselves suggest. You should avoid sending mixed messages. Keep the tone of your voice consistent with the words you use. And don't say something one day and contradict it the next; players will get their wires crossed.

You also want to keep your terminology consistent. Many volleyball terms describe the same or similar skills. Take the team's third contact, for example. One coach may use the term "attack it," while another coach may say to "spike it" or "terminate it." Although all these are correct, to be consistent as a staff, the coaches of a team should agree on all terms before the start of the season, teach those terms to the team, and then stay with them.

Nonverbal Messages

Just as you should be consistent in the tone of voice and words you use, you should also keep your verbal and nonverbal messages consistent. An extreme example of failing to do this would be shaking your head, indicating disapproval, while at the same time telling a player "Nice try." Which is the player to believe, your gesture or your words?

Messages can be sent nonverbally in several ways. Facial expressions and body language are just two of the more obvious forms of nonverbal signals that can help you when you coach. Keep in mind that as a coach you need to be a teacher first, and any action that detracts from the message you are trying to convey should be avoided.

Facial Expressions

The look on a person's face is the quickest clue to what the person thinks or feels. Your players know this, so they will study your face, looking for a sign that will tell them more than the words you say. Don't try to fool them by putting on a happy or blank "mask." They'll see through it, and you'll lose credibility.

Serious, stone-faced expressions provide no cues to kids who want to know how they are performing. When faced with this, kids will just assume you're unhappy or disinterested. Don't be afraid to smile. A smile from a coach can give a great boost to an unsure player. Plus, a smile lets your players know that you are happy and confident when coaching them. But don't overdo it, or your players won't be able to tell when you are genuinely pleased by something they've done or when you are just putting on a smiling face.

Body Language

What would your players think you were feeling if you came to practice slouched over, with your head down and your shoulders slumped? Would they think you were tired, bored, or unhappy? What would they think you were feeling if you watched them during a game with your hands on your hips, your jaws clenched, and your face frowning and red? Would they think you were upset with them, disgusted at an official, or mad at a fan? Probably some or all of these things would enter your players' minds. And none is the impression you want your players to have of you. That's why you should carry yourself in a pleasant, confident, and enthusiastic manner.

Physical contact can also be a very important use of body language. A high five, a pat on the head, an arm around the shoulder, and even a big hug are effective ways to show approval, concern, affection, and joy to your players. Youngsters are especially in need of this type of nonverbal message. Keep within the obvious moral and legal limits, of course, but don't be reluctant to use appropriate touch to send a message that can only be expressed in that way.

Coaching Tip

As a coach, you need to be aware of your body language. Players of all ages will pick up on your actions and habits, so you must ensure that you provide a good example for your players to model. All it takes is a few eye rolls or wild hand gestures to send a message that this type of behavior is acceptable, even if that would never be your intent.

Improving Your Receiving Skills

Now let's examine the other half of the communication process: receiving messages. Too often very good senders are very poor receivers of messages. But as a coach of young players, you must be able to fulfill both roles effectively.

The requirements for receiving messages are quite simple, but receiving skills are perhaps less satisfying and therefore underdeveloped compared to sending skills. People seem to enjoy hearing themselves talk more than they enjoy hearing others talk. But if you learn the keys to receiving messages and make a strong effort to use them with your players, you'll be surprised by what you've been missing.

Pay Attention

First, you must pay attention; you must want to hear what others have to communicate to you. That's not always easy when you're busy coaching and have many things competing for your attention. But in one-on-one or team meetings with players, you must focus on what they are telling you, both verbally and nonverbally. You'll be amazed at the little signals you pick up. Not only will this focused attention help you catch every word your players say, but you'll also notice your players' moods and physical states. In addition, you'll get an idea of your players' feelings toward you and other players on the team.

Listen Carefully

How you receive messages from others, perhaps more than anything else you do, demonstrates how much you care for the sender and what that person has to tell you. If you care little for your players or have little regard for what they have to say, it will show in how you attend and listen to them. You need to check yourself. Do you find your mind wandering to what you are going to do after practice while one of your players is talking to you? Do you frequently have to ask your players, "What did you say?" If so, you need to work on your receiving mechanics of attending and listening. Asking questions for clarification shows that you are listening and care about what the players are saying. But if you find that you're missing the messages your players send, perhaps the most critical question you should ask yourself is this: "Do I care enough to be a coach?"

Providing Feedback

So far we've discussed separately the sending and receiving of messages. But we all know that senders and receivers switch roles several times during an interaction. One person initiates a communication by sending a message to another person, who then receives the message. The receiver then becomes the sender by responding to the person who sent the initial message. These verbal and nonverbal responses are called *feedback*.

Your players will look to you for feedback all the time. They will want to know how you think they are performing, what you think of their ideas, and whether their efforts please you. You can respond in many different ways, and how you respond will strongly affect your players. They will react most favorably to positive feedback.

Praising players when they have performed or behaved well is an effective way of getting them to repeat (or try to repeat) that behavior. And positive feedback for effort is an especially effective way to motivate youngsters to work on difficult skills. So rather than shouting at and providing negative feedback to players who have made mistakes, you should try offering positive feedback and letting them know what they did correctly (catch them doing it right) and how they can improve. Praise in a loud voice for all to hear, and if giving negative feedback, do it individually and softly. In other words, you should shout praise and whisper criticism. Sometimes just the way you word feedback can make it more positive than negative. For example, instead of saying, "Don't hit the ball that way," you might say, "Hit the ball this way." Then your players will be focusing on what to do instead of what not to do.

Positive feedback can be verbal or nonverbal. Telling young players, especially in front of teammates, that they have performed well is a great way to boost their confidence. And a pat on the back or a high five communicates that you recognize a player's effort and performance.

Communicating With Other Groups

In addition to sending and receiving messages and providing proper feedback to players, coaching also involves interacting with members of the coaching staff, parents, fans, officials, and opposing coaches. If you don't communicate effectively with these groups, your coaching career will be unpleasant and short lived. So try the following suggestions for communicating with these groups.

Coaching Staff

Before you hold your first practice, the coaching staff should meet and discuss the roles and responsibilities that each coach will undertake during the year. Depending on the number of assistant coaches, the staff responsibilities can be divided into different areas. For example, one coach may be in charge of working with the setters while another is responsible for helping players work on the attack. The head coach has the final responsibility for all phases of the game, but as much as possible, the assistant coaches should be responsible for their areas.

Before practices start, the coaching staff must also discuss and agree on terminology, plans for practice, game day organization, the method of communicating during practice and games, and how to handle specific game conditions. The coaches on your staff must present a united front and speak with one voice, and they must all take a similar approach to coaching, interaction with the players and parents, and interaction with one another. Disagreements should be discussed away from the court, and each coach should have a say as the staff comes to an agreement.

Parents

A player's parents need to be assured that their child is under the direction of a coach who is both knowledgeable about the sport and concerned about the youngster's well-being. You can put their worries to rest by holding a preseason parent-orientation meeting in which you describe your background and your approach to coaching. See "Preseason Meeting Topics" for a sample outline of information to cover at a parent-orientation meeting. (Note that the type of paperwork needed before the season starts, as well as the procedures and costs for handing out or purchasing equipment, will vary by team and league.)

Preseason Meeting Topics

1. Share your coaching philosophy.

2. Outline the paperwork that is needed, such as:
   - Copy of the player's birth certificate
   - Completed player's application and payment record
   - Report card from the previous year
   - Participation agreement form
   - Physical exam form
   - Informed consent form
   - Emergency information card

3. Go over the inherent risks of volleyball and other safety issues. Review your emergency action plan.

4. Inform parents of procedures related to uniforms and equipment, including what items the league or team will provide and what equipment players must furnish themselves.

5. Review the season practice schedule, including the date, location, and time of each practice.

6. Go over the proper gear and attire that should be worn at each practice session.

7. Discuss nutrition, hydration, and rest for players.

8. Explain the goals for the team.

9. Cover methods of communication: e-mail list, emergency phone numbers, interactive Web site, and so on.

10. Discuss ways that parents can help with the team. Solicit volunteers.

11. Discuss standards of conduct for coaches, players, and parents.

12. Provide time for questions and answers.

If parents contact you with a concern during the season, you should listen to them closely and try to offer positive responses. Parents may sometimes want to talk to you about their child immediately after a game or practice, which can be an emotionally charged situation. If this occurs, you should encourage the parents to make an appointment to discuss their concerns with you at a later time, when everyone will be much calmer. If you need to communicate with parents, you can catch them after a practice or game, give them a phone call, or send a note through e-mail or regular mail. Messages sent to parents through players are too often lost, misinterpreted, or forgotten.

Fans

The stands probably won't be overflowing at your games, which means that you'll more easily hear the few fans who criticize your coaching. When you hear something negative about the job you're doing, don't respond. Keep calm, consider whether the message had any value, and if not, forget it. Acknowledging critical, unwarranted comments from a fan during a game will only encourage others to voice their opinions. So put away your "rabbit ears" and communicate to fans, through your actions, that you are a confident, competent coach.

You must also prepare your players for fans' criticisms. Tell your players that it is you, not the spectators or the parents in the stands, that they should listen to. If you notice that one of your players is rattled by a fan's comment, you should reassure the player that your evaluation is more objective and favorable—and the one that counts.

Officials

How you communicate with officials will have a great influence on the way your players behave toward them. Therefore, you must set a good example.

Greet officials with a handshake, an introduction, and perhaps casual conversation about the upcoming contest. Indicate your respect for them before, during, and after the game. Don't shout, make nasty remarks, or use disrespectful body gestures. Your players will see you do it, and they'll get the idea that such behavior is appropriate. Plus, if the official hears or sees you, the communication between the two of you will break down.

Opposing Coaches

Make an effort to visit with the coach of the opposing team before the game. During the game, don't get into a personal feud with the opposing coach. Remember, it's the kids, not the coaches, who are competing. And by getting along well with the opposing coach, you'll show your players that competition involves cooperation.

3

Understanding Rules and Equipment

Volleyball is unique in that it is a game of errors where the objective is to get the ball to hit the floor on the opponent's side of the net or force the opponent to make a ballhandling error. Thus, the majority of points scored in volleyball are the result of an error. Although the concept is simple, specific offensive and defensive aspects of the game are executed differently based on the level of play and the game situation all governed by a thick rule

Age Modifications for Volleyball

Before we begin, let's consider some of the modifications that can be made to accommodate different age groups. Things such as the size of the court, the size of the ball, and the duration of the game, along with some playing rules, can be adjusted for the various age groups to help accommodate players' development and skill levels. The following table outlines basic modifications for championship play as recommended by USA Volleyball. Local leagues are encouraged to follow or modify these rules as they deem appropriate for the ages and skill levels of the players.

	Ages 6 to 9	Ages 10 to 11	Ages 12 to 14
Roster size	4-5	6-7	9-10
Players on court	3v3	4v4	6v6
Ball	Beach balls, "gator" balls, oversized (#6), or light (#5)	Oversized (#6) or light (#5)	Light (#5) for age 12 and regular ball for age 13 and up
Court size	On a regulation volleyball court, two 3v3 courts are set up on each side, with a length of 4 meters and a width of 4 meters (may also be increased to 4.5, 6, or even 9 meters). The courts begin 2 meters inside the end line and there is a 2-meter buffer in between each court's sideline (see figure 3.1c).	On a regulation volleyball court, two 4v4 courts are set up using the sidelines for a 4- or 5-meter-long court or basketball court sidelines for a 6-meter-long court. The width is from the regulation volleyball court's end line to the attack line (see figure 3.1b).	Regulation court (see figure 3.1a).
Net height	6 ft.	6 ft. 6 in.	7 ft. for age 12; 7 ft. 4 1/8 in. for age 13 and up

book. This introduction to the basic rules of volleyball won't cover every rule of the game but instead will give you what you need to work with players who are 6 to 14 years old. In this chapter, we cover the basics of the game, such as the number of players, equipment, and court size depending on your team's age group. We also describe specifics such as player positions, game procedures, and rules of play. We wrap things up by describing officiating and identifying some of the most common referee signals.

Court

The court that the game is played on varies depending on the age level of your players, the number of players on the court, the lines already available on the floor of the court, the court surface, and whether the court is indoors or outdoors. At the youth level, games are typically played indoors on hard surfaces or outdoors on hard (asphalt, concrete), grass, or sand surfaces. The game has even been played on mud or snow as part of fund-raising or charity events. Because of the various types of surfaces that volleyball can be played on, an actual "court" is not always required as in other sports. Your league may give you the freedom to create the type of court that you need for your program.

All lines marking the playing area on hard courts are two inches wide. For 6v6 play, games are typically played on full-size standard volleyball courts, and the court lines will already be in place, as shown in figure 3.1a. Younger age groups often play on smaller, modified courts; many leagues use the existing lines on a full-size court to create a standard court size for their league, as shown in figures 3.1b and 3.1c. The modified court sizes help make the game more playable for younger and smaller players. On the smaller courts, the players don't have to run as far, and they have more opportunities for contact with the ball. Modified court sizes are not just for the youth level; you even see them at the Olympic level, where the beach game of 2v2 uses a court that is a full meter (3 feet) smaller than the regulation indoor 9-by-18-meter (59 by 29 1/2 feet) court.

If court dimensions aren't already marked or need to be modified, there are several ways you can set up your own court. For indoor surfaces, special floor-safe tape, cones, or markers can be used. Two youth courts are commonly set up so that they share one regulation net, with a 2-meter buffer in between (see figure 3.2). If you have access to adult badminton, tennis, racquetball, or squash courts, you can set up youth volleyball courts on these. For example, on a regulation badminton court, 3v3 volleyball can be played using the singles court (or 4v4 using the doubles court) with extenders on the standards to get the net to volleyball height. Or, on a regulation racquetball court, 4v4 volleyball can be played using the whole court with the walls as the boundaries (or 3v3 by shortening the end lines [front and back walls] to 4.5 meters), again using extenders to raise the net to volleyball height.

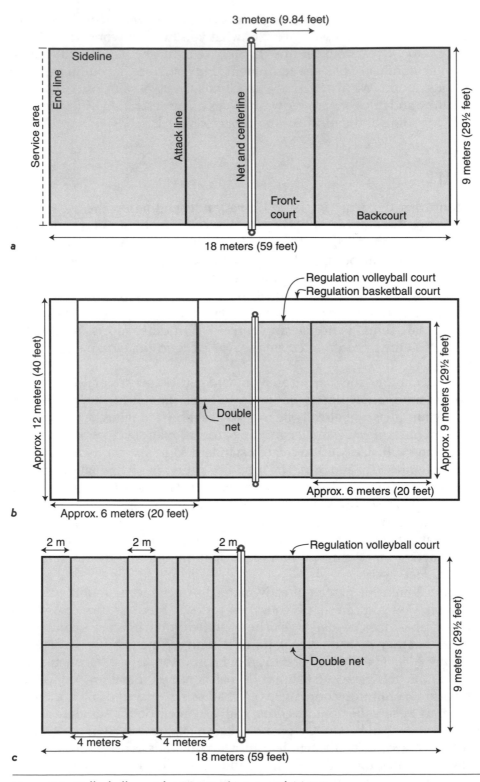

Figure 3.1 Volleyball court for *(a)* 6v6, *(b)* 4v4, and *(c)* 3v3.

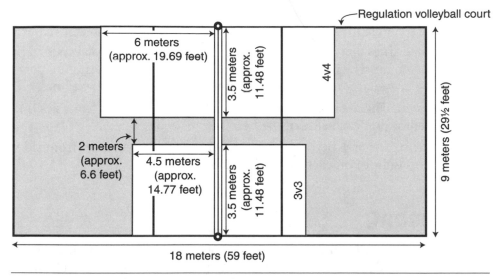

Figure 3.2 Two youth courts on one regulation court.

For outdoor play on grass or sand courts, you can mark the playing area using rope secured with stakes, sand anchors, or other similar items. Cones or markers can also be used. On grass, court lines may be designated using spray paint rather than ropes. Note that for youth volleyball up through 4v4, courts do not need an attack line because all players, whether in the front row or back row, are allowed to attack the ball (as discussed in "Rules of Play" on page 31). For 6v6 play, however, the attack line is used and should be marked 3 meters (9 feet 9 inches) from the net on each side of the court (as shown in figure 3.1). On indoor courts, you can designate the attack lines using floor-safe tape if these lines do not already exist. However, it is not common to mark an attack line on grass or beach surfaces (although the attack line can be spray painted on grass).

Several areas of the courts shown in figures 3.1 and 3.2 are referred to with special volleyball terminology. Here are a few definitions:

- *Service area.* The area behind the end line and between the extension of the two sidelines from where the ball may be served.

- *Attack line.* A line on the court 3 meters (9 feet 9 inches) from and parallel to the net on each side that delineates the frontcourt from the backcourt. When the attack line is used (in 6v6 play), back-row players may not jump and attack the ball with their hands above the top of the net from in front of this line. The attack line is also referred to as the *10-foot line* or the *3-meter line*.

- *Centerline.* A line that runs parallel to and directly under the net from sideline to sideline. This line marks the center of the court and separates the two playing areas. Players may step on but not completely over this line during play as long as they do not interfere with the opponent's ability to play the ball.

- *End line.* A line that is parallel to the net at the back of each playing area. While serving, players must stay behind this line until contact is made.
- *Sidelines.* Lines that mark the sides of each playing area. All players, except the server, must be inside these lines at the time of service. After the serve has been contacted, players may pursue balls outside of these lines.
- *Frontcourt.* The area between the attack line and the net (from sideline to sideline) on each side of the net.
- *Backcourt.* The area between the attack line and the end line (from sideline to sideline) on each side of the net.

Equipment

The standard pieces of equipment for volleyball include balls, nets and antennae, standards and padding, knee pads, and appropriate apparel. But how do you know when this equipment meets proper specifications and is in good repair? As a coach, you must examine the condition of each item you distribute to players. Also make sure that the pieces of equipment they furnish themselves meet acceptable standards. You should ensure that each player on your team is outfitted properly, and you may need to demonstrate to players how to properly wear their equipment. Following is additional information on the common equipment used in volleyball:

Ball

Standards for volleyballs as recommended by USA Volleyball are noted in "Age Modifications for Volleyball" on page 22, but your local league may also have specific requirements for the balls that you use. To introduce skills and vary the learning environment during practices, you can experiment with the use of punch balloons, beach balls, or rubber-bladder balls. Ideally, each player should have her own legal volleyball so that she can become more familiar with the weight and feel of the ball. This also makes it easy for players to practice at home.

Net

A regulation volleyball net is commonly used in youth play. The net is attached to poles, called *standards*, that are placed three feet outside of the playing area. For youth play (as opposed to higher levels), your league may give you the flexibility to create a net if you do not have access to a real volleyball net. For example, you can use ropes or badminton nets by raising them to volleyball height. Whatever the form, you must regularly inspect all equipment for wear and tear, loose or sharp parts, and other defects, and you must replace or repair the equipment as necessary. The standards used to hold the net should be securely anchored and should be padded for safety. In beach play, net antennae are not normally used, but for indoor play, antennae should be securely placed on the net and should be regularly inspected for defects. Bicycle safety flags attached to the net over the sidelines of the court, or floor tape placed on the net, can be good substitutes for official net antennae.

Knee Pads

The use of knee pads on grass or beach surfaces is allowed, but knee pads are typically worn for games played on hard surfaces in order to make it easier for players to tolerate hitting the floor. Knee pads are made of foam or rubber covered with a soft elastic material. The pads should fit snugly. For younger players, soft-surface elbow pads such as those worn in many youth contact sports may actually fit better when used as a knee pad.

Apparel

At the youth level, most practice and competition uniforms are as simple as shorts and T-shirts. For practices, you may permit your players to wear whatever they choose as long as the clothing is unrestricting and allows the player to move freely. When considering game uniforms, however, you must first check with your league, because some leagues require a team to wear matching shirts and shorts. Your league may also require the team jerseys to be numbered. Typically, a smaller number should be placed in the upper center of the front of the jersey, with a larger number in the upper center of the back of the jersey. The color of the numbers should be in contrast to the jersey color so the numbers can be easily seen.

During both practices and games, players should wear a type of athletic shoe that is comfortable, supports the arch, and cushions the heel and the ball of the foot. Shoes should be broken in before they're worn during intense activity. Volleyball or court shoes are fine for playing on hard courts. Running shoes are not recommended, however, because they don't give lateral support to the foot. When playing on grassy or beach surfaces, some players choose to wear shoes, while others prefer to play barefoot. Many beach players play in socks to protect the feet from heat exposure or burning from the sand.

Special Equipment

Players may be able to participate while wearing casts, braces, splints, or prostheses, as long as any hard, exposed surfaces are covered and padded. In this situation, the player should be cleared to play by a doctor, and the equipment should be inspected and approved by the game official.

Player Positions

At the youth level, volleyball is typically played 3v3 for the 6- to 9-year age group, 4v4 for the 10- to 11-year age group, and 6v6 for the 12- to 14-year age group. In the following sections, we describe the basic player positions when starting a match for each of these versions of the game.

Coaching Tip
Younger players or those new to the sport need to work on developing all the basic skills of volleyball without specializing in any one position on the court. Many times, because of differences in physical, mental, or social maturity, young players are pushed into specialized roles (the tallest players are taught only to block and hit; the shortest players are expected only to pass and set) only to find later in their careers that other roles are more appropriate for them. At youth levels, all players must develop the fundamental skills of volleyball (serving, passing, setting, hitting, individual defense, and blocking) to play the game effectively.

Positions for 3v3

For 3v3 volleyball, the players are positioned in a triangle formation where one player is in the frontcourt (the front half of the court) and two players split the backcourt (the back half of the court), as shown in figure 3.3. The responsibilities of these three players are as follows:

- *Position A (passer).* This position is considered the first contact position; the player in this position initiates the start of play with a serve on offense and makes first contact on balls coming over the net from the opponent. This player will become the secondary setter if the player in position B (the primary setter) receives the first ball over the net. The player in position A may also become a secondary hitter if the player in position C is not in position to attack or if the setter (player B) chooses to set to player A.

- *Position B (setter).* The player in this position is the primary setter on offense and the primary blocker on defense. This player should always strive to make the second contact (the set to the attacker). However, this player may become a secondary attacker if the player in position C (the primary attacker) makes the second contact and sets the ball for one of the other players to attack.

- *Position C (hitter).* The player in this position will make most of the third contacts and is considered the primary attacker on offense and the primary digger on defense. This player may become the secondary setter if the first contact is made by the player in position A or B.

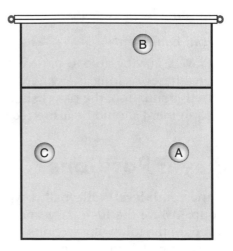

Figure 3.3   Basic positions for 3v3 play.

Positions for 4v4

For 4v4 volleyball, the players are positioned with one player in the front row and three players in the back row, as shown in figure 3.4. The responsibilities of these four players are as follows:

- *Position A (right-back passer or hitter).* This position may be considered the first contact position; the player in this position will initiate the start of play with a serve on offense and may also make first contact on balls coming over the net from the opponent. This player may become the secondary setter if the player in position B (the primary setter) receives the first ball over the net on defense.

- *Position B (center-front setter).* The player in this position is the primary setter on offense and the primary blocker on defense. This player should always strive to make the second contact (the set to one of the attackers). However, this player may become a secondary attacker if she plays the first ball over the net and another player can set to her for the third contact.

- *Position C (left-back passer or hitter).* The player in this position is a primary attacker on offense and will make many of the third contacts for the team. This player is also a primary crosscourt digger on defense. This player may become a secondary setter if the served or attacked ball is played by the player in position B and the player in position A is unable to set the second contact.

- *Position D (center-back passer or hitter).* The player in this position is a secondary attacker on offense. This player is also a secondary crosscourt digger and may take many of the first contacts on defense or on serve receive. This player may occasionally become a secondary setter if the player in position B cannot take the second contact and neither player in positions A or C can step in to make that contact.

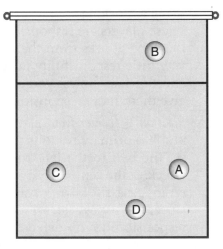

Figure 3.4   Basic positions for 4v4 play.

Positions for 6v6

For a 6v6 match, the basic positions include three front-row and three back-row players, as shown in figure 3.5. The responsibilities of these six players are as follows:

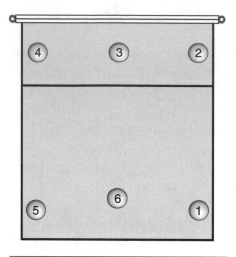

Figure 3.5   Basic positions for 6v6 play.

- *Position 1 (right-back player).* When the team rotates, the player who moves into this position is the server. After she serves, this player will move into the court to become a defensive player. When the opponent serves, the player in this position will have primary serve-receive responsibility. Following the serve-reception pass and the set for an attack, this player will move forward to the area in front of the attack line on the right side of the court. This will enable her to cover any ball that is blocked by the opponent after being attacked by the hitter in the right-front position. Then, assuming the ball crosses the net into the opponent's court and is kept in play by the opponent, the right-back player becomes a defensive player once more.

- *Position 2 (right-front player)* and *position 4 (left-front player).* The players in these positions are primary attackers on offense, and if the team is using a blocking alignment, they are also primary blockers on defense. These players are responsible for attacking sets made by the setter and blocking attacks from the opponent's hitters. These players may have very little responsibility in serve reception (other than for short front-court serves), unless you choose to modify serve-reception patterns to give them more responsibility.

- *Position 3 (center-front player).* The player in this position is the setter and has primary responsibility for the second contact. This player will set the ball to the left-front and right-front players, allowing for an attack. If the center-front player is unable to set the ball because of an errant pass, she is responsible for calling for help so that another player closer to the pass can set to a hitter. This player may also have blocking responsibilities on defense; she may assist the left-front or right-front player in executing a double block, or she may block by herself against an attack from the middle zone of the net.

- *Position 5 (left-back player).* The player in this position has primary serve-receive responsibility as well as primary crosscourt digging responsibility on defense against the opponent's left-front hitter. Following serve reception, similar to the player in position 1 (right back), this player will move forward in front of the attack line to cover any ball that may be blocked by the opponent after being attacked by the hitter on her side of the court (left front). Then, assuming the ball crosses the net into the opponent's court and is kept in play by the opponent, the left-back player becomes a defensive player once more.

- *Position 6 (center-back player).* The player in this position will have primary defensive responsibility for digging hits from the opponent's left-front and right-front attackers. This player may also have primary serve-reception responsibility, depending on the type of serve-reception alignment used (see chapter 8 for more information on serve-reception alignments).

Rules of Play

Volleyball rules are designed to make the game run smoothly and safely and to prevent either team from gaining an unfair advantage. Throw out the rules and a volleyball game can quickly turn chaotic. Following is an overview of some of the basic rules in volleyball.

Starting a Match

Before a match, one player from each team will participate in a coin toss that determines which team will serve first in game 1. The winner of the toss will choose to serve first or will choose which side of the court her team will start on. The loser of the toss will get the remaining choice. After switching sides of the court, game 2 of the match will be started with a serve by the team that did not serve first in game 1. For the third or deciding game, another coin toss will be held to determine the serving team. The teams will switch sides of the net at the halfway point of the deciding game (8 points) and will continue play of the game from their same rotational positions.

Player Lineups

A few minutes before match time (usually after the coin toss), the coach must submit a written lineup of the team's starting players to the referee and the scorekeeper (this is done before each game of a match). This lineup will list all eligible players and their uniform numbers (you may also be asked to indicate the floor captain on the lineup), plus a diagram of the court with the numbers of your starting players in the positions that they will start the game in. The lineup that you submit determines the rotation of players throughout the game—called the *serving order*—and helps the referee and scorekeeper know if players are in their correct rotational order before each serve.

It is up to the coach to make decisions on where to place players in the lineup. Some coaches may choose to always start a game with their strongest server in the right-back (first server) position; some may choose to start with their strongest setter and blockers in the front row. Essentially, the coach needs to be aware of the opponent's strengths and weaknesses in order to place players in the best positions to counteract those strengths and take advantage of those weaknesses. See "Starting and Substituting Players" on page 141 in chapter 9 for more information.

Serving Order and Player Rotation

During play, players of both teams must be in their correct rotational order, or serving order, at the time of the contact by either team (as designated on the lineup as discussed in the previous section). If players are not in their correct serving order at the time of service, they may be called for being *out of rotation* or for *overlapping*. The correct positioning of each player at the time of service for 3v3, 4v4, and 6v6 play is described as follows:

- In 3v3 play, the player in position B must be in front of the players in positions A and C, and the player in position A must be to the right of the player in position C.

- In 4v4 play, the player in position B (or second in the serving order) must be in front of the players in positions A, C, and D. The player in position A (the serving position) must be to the right of the player in position D (last in the serving order). The player in position D must be to the right of the player in position C and to the left of the player in position A.

- In 6v6 play, the center-front player must be between the right-front and left-front players and in front of the center-back player. The center-back player must be between the right-back and left-back players and behind the center-front player. The right-front player must be in front of the right-back player, and the left-front player must be in front of the left-back player.

When a player is out of position, the referee stops play, the error is corrected, any points scored while the team was in error are canceled, and a point (and the serve) is awarded to the opponent. After the ball is contacted on the serve, players may move to any court position they wish during the rally, but they must always return to the correct rotational order before the next serve.

When their team obtains the serve, players rotate one position clockwise. For example, on a six-player team, the player in the right-front position will rotate back to become the server, the previous server will rotate to her left to the center-back position, and so on (see figure 3.6).

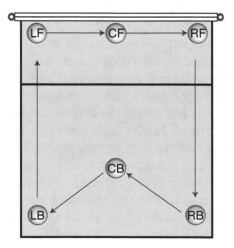

Figure 3.6   Clockwise rotation for a six-player team.

Serving

The player who starts in the right-back position or rotates into that position on the serving team will initiate the serve for her team. When the official blows the whistle for the serve, the server has eight seconds to serve the ball. If the ball is not contacted within the eight seconds, the official stops play and awards the ball and a point to the opponent. The server may move freely in the service area, which runs the entire width of the court along the end line (as shown in figure 3.1 on page 24); however, she must be completely in the service zone and must not be touching the playing surface, which includes all court lines or their extensions (sidelines), at the moment of contact (or at takeoff for serves that include a jump).

In most youth league play, a player is allowed one service tossing error (letting the ball bounce without hitting it after tossing it up for a serve) per serve attempt—that is, the player is still allowed to serve after this occurs. But a serve fault results in the loss of serve and a point to the opponent. A serve fault occurs when the serve touches a player of the serving team, fails to pass over the net, hits the net antennae or fails to pass between the net antennae, lands out of bounds, or passes over a screen. Note that a served ball is considered to be in play if it touches the top of the net during the serve and falls into the opponent's court.

If the serving team wins the rally, the player who served on that point (or her substitute, if applicable) will serve again. If the receiving team wins the rally, it gains the right to serve and rotates one position clockwise.

Ball Contact

Legal contact is a touch of the ball by any part of the player's body that does not allow the ball to visibly come to rest or involve prolonged contact with a player's body. The USAV requirements for legal contact state that the ball may contact any part of the body and any number of body parts as long as it does so simultaneously. If the contact of more than one body part is not simultaneous, a *double contact* violation will occur, resulting in a point (and the ball) being awarded to the opponent. Some other types of ball contact—such as catching, holding, throwing, lifting, or pushing the ball—are considered illegal and result in a violation called *illegal contact*. (See "Violations" on page 36 for more information.)

After the serve has been made and during the rally, each team may take up to three contacts to return the ball to the opponent's court. After an opponent's attack, if the first touch by the defensive team is a block, the team will be allowed three additional contacts after the block to return the ball. Note that in youth volleyball up through 4v4, all players are allowed to attack the ball, and the attack line is not used (see "Net Play" on page 34 for more information).

A double contact violation occurs when one player hits the ball more than once with no other player touching it between these contacts, or when one player contacts the ball in succession with two body parts (as described previously). However, a player who blocks the ball may touch it a second time without an intervening touch by another player. Simultaneous contact occurs when two players on the same team contact the ball at exactly the same time; this is counted as one contact for the team, and either player is allowed to make the next contact (if one or more contacts remain). If two teammates contact the ball on a block attempt, it is counted as only one hit for their team, and the team has three additional contacts available to them. The same is true when two opposing players contact the ball at exactly the same time on a block or hit above the net—whichever side the ball falls into, that team gets three additional contacts.

Net Play

As with serving, when in play, the ball must pass from one side of the net to the other over the legal portion of the net completely between the net antennae. The ball may touch the net as it passes back and forth; however, players contacting the ball at the net may not touch the net (some types of hits will result in a violation called a *net fault*; for more information, see "Violations" on page 36).

According to USAV rules, a player may not touch the net during play except for insignificant contact by a player not in the act of playing the ball. Players can, however, cross the vertical plane (an imaginary continuation of the net above and below its actual limits) as long as they don't interfere with an opponent. In addition, the feet are the only part of the body allowed to touch the opponent's court (at least part of one foot must remain on or above the centerline at the time of contact). A player who places any part of her body above the height of the net is automatically considered to have the intention to block. A block is only legal on a ball that is hit in such a manner that it would clearly cross the net if not touched by a defending player. If a ball is not clearly crossing the net (such as when a set is traveling toward a hitter) and it is blocked, this would result in an illegal block.

In 6v6 play, only front-row players may block, and only front-row players are allowed to spike or return the ball with their hands in a position higher than the top of the net when they are in front of the attack line. Back-row players may not block at all and may spike only when they take off (jump) from completely behind the attack line. A player may not spike the ball until part of the ball is on that player's side of the net. The player's hands may legally pass over the net on the follow-through after a spike.

Scoring

Various scoring methods can be used in volleyball. You should check with your league to find out which method is required or recommended. The two most common methods at the youth level are rally scoring and timed games:

Rally Scoring

Most youth volleyball leagues—as well as leagues for all ages and abilities—use rally scoring and a best-of-three game format. This is also the type of scoring recommended by USA Volleyball. In rally scoring, a point is scored on every serve, no matter which team served. The team who wins the point gets to serve the next point. For example, team A serves the ball out of bounds, so team B gets the point and the next serve. This is the only format in which the nonserving team can score points. It makes the length of most games shorter than the more traditional side-out scoring method where only the serving team could score a point.

Timed Games

Timed games may be used in large youth tournaments or in round-robin competition at any level. With this method, time is limited in order to keep the competition running smoothly. Timed games commonly use rally scoring, and the team with the most points when time runs out is the winner of the game. Depending on the number of teams and courts available, 8- to 10-minute games—with teams changing sides of the court at the end of the second game and at the midpoint of the third game—are typical.

Substitutions

Your league may have specific rules regarding substitutions, but in general, every player must play at least half of each competition. Although the substitution rules for higher levels are relatively strict, for youth games these rules are modified to ensure that each player gets the opportunity to participate. The most common substitution method is to use a circular rotation where substitutes rotate into the game at either the serving spot or the front-row spot. (See "Starting and Substituting Players" on page 141 of chapter 9 for more information on methods of substituting during a game.)

Substitutions can only be made during a dead ball. Typically, you are limited to three entries per player (your league may also have limits on how many total team substitutions you may make during one single game). A player coming into the game will stand at the sideline (between the attack line and the net) and face the player she is replacing. When recognized by the official, the players will change places, and the player going into the game will take the position on the court where the player leaving the game was positioned.

In 6v6 play, one designated player, called a *libero*, is allowed unlimited substitution into the back row for any back-row player. Essentially, liberos are considered to be back-row specialists whose responsibilities include serve-receive passing and playing defense against the opponent's attackers. The libero may not serve (except in the cases of some collegiate and high school rules), play the front row to attack or block, or set to a hitter using an overhead pass (forearm passes are okay) when the libero is in front of the attack line. Additionally, liberos may not attack and make contact with the ball from above the top of the net when in the back row. You should check with your local league for more information about the use of this specialty position.

Time-Outs

At all levels of play, each team is allowed two time-outs per game. Time-outs last 30 seconds (they may be taken one at a time or in immediate succession). Time-outs may be requested by the coach or by the team captain on the floor. Time-outs are usually requested in order to communicate strategy to your players; to break the other team's rhythm, concentration, or momentum; or to interrupt a strong server. Time-outs may be taken on any dead ball during the game or before the first serve of the game. When the request for a time-out is acknowledged by the official's whistle, all players should leave the court and gather near their team bench for instructions. When the official blows the whistle to indicate the end of the time-out, all players in the game before the time-out must reenter the court immediately; if they waste time or are slow getting back on the court, they may be called for a delay of game penalty, resulting in a point for the opponent.

Violations

Violations of the playing rules will often result in the award of serve and a point to the opponent. Here are some of the more common violations that may be observed at the youth level:

- *Held ball.* This occurs when the ball momentarily comes to rest in the hands or on the arms of a player. The penalty for a held ball is a point to the other team, and they are also awarded the serve if they were the receiving team.

- *Double fault.* If the ball is "held" (see *held ball*) simultaneously by two opposing players, it is a double fault and results in a playover. In a playover, no point is awarded, and the same server will serve the ball again so the point or rally is replayed.

- *Serve fault.* A serve fault occurs when the served ball touches a player of the serving team, fails to pass over the net, fails to pass completely between the net antennae (or their extensions), lands out of bounds, or passes over a screen (when one or more players wave arms, jump, or move sideways, hiding the server as the ball is being served). This should not be confused with a service line fault (see *line violation*) in which the server contacts or steps over the service line before contacting the ball.

- *Net fault.* This occurs any time a player contacts the net or its supports while in the act of playing the ball. For this violation, a point and the serve are awarded to the opponent. Incidental contact with the net by a player not involved in the play is not considered a fault. Also, if the ball is driven into the net with such force that the net contacts an opponent, this is not considered a net fault on the opponent.

- *Line violation.* A line violation occurs if a player steps on or over the attack line when jumping and attacking from the back row; if a player steps on or over the sideline or end line when serving; or if a player steps completely across the centerline under the net when blocking, attacking, or digging a ball. It is also a line violation for any player on the court to step on or outside of the sidelines or end lines before the server contacts the ball on the serve. Any of these situations result in a point and the serve being awarded to the opponent.

- *Illegal block.* An illegal block occurs when a back-row player blocks at the net, when a player blocks the opponent's serve, or when a player reaches over the net to contact a ball that is not traveling toward the net. An illegal block will also be called when a player blocks a ball before the attacker has a chance to attempt to hit the team's third contact. If an illegal block occurs, the opponent is awarded a point and the serve.

Volleyball No-Nos

It's inevitable that your players will violate minor rules during practices and games. But you must make it clear to your players that some actions are unacceptable on the volleyball court and can result in an individual or team penalty, depending on the severity of the infraction. Here are some examples:

- Making rude or vulgar remarks or gestures
- Engaging in disruptive or distracting behavior on the bench during the game
- Shouting or clapping at an opponent who is playing or attempting to play a ball
- Shouting or swearing in anger, even at your own play
- Questioning a judgment call of an official
- Talking to the officials (only the coach and captain may address the officials)
- Throwing, slamming, or kicking the ball in anger

Your role as a coach is not limited to teaching fundamentals; you must also promote good sporting behavior both on and off the court. For example, encourage your players to call their own net violations and touches on the ball; to help teammates up off the floor after the ball has been called dead; to compliment a teammate or an opponent on a great play; to roll the ball under the net to the other team at the end of a rally; and to run to retrieve any dead balls and return them to the server or the official. Both your opponents and the officials will appreciate this behavior.

Officials

Officials enforce the rules of the game. For 6v6 play at the youth level, there are usually two officials (for 3v3 or 4v4 play, there may be only one official). The first referee—also called the *up official*—is positioned at the sideline on the opposite side from the team benches and is usually on an elevated platform (so that the referee's eye level is above the top of the net). This official directs the match from start to finish; he or she is responsible for whistling and signaling for service, for the end of the rally, and for all violations. The up official also authorizes or rejects team requests. If there is a second referee—called the *down official*—he or she is positioned on the floor facing the first referee on the same side of the court as the team benches. This second official is the assistant to the first referee. The responsibilities of the second official include signaling (and whistling on some) any observed faults, controlling the scorers and the team benches, and managing the called time-outs and substitutions. Line judges may also be used in the match to help the officials call balls in and out. If used, line judges will be stationed at opposite diagonal corners of the court, one on each team's end line (at the sideline closest to each referee's right hand) to call balls on the sideline and end line. Line judges also help call touches on out balls, balls outside or touching the antennae, and foot faults on the server. See figure 3.7 for common officiating signals used at the youth level.

The scorekeeper will record the official starting lineups of each team and will keep the official scorebook. If the scorekeeper has an assistant, that person will usually operate the visible scoring device. The assistant may also track the entries of the libero for each team on a tracking form. The scorekeeper will track team substitutions and time-outs, and he or she will notify the officials if someone is out of serving order. If there is a discrepancy between the visible score and the scorebook, the scorebook is considered the official score, and the visible device should be corrected. The scorekeeper's table should be located outside the sideline near the net, on the opposite side of the court from the first referee.

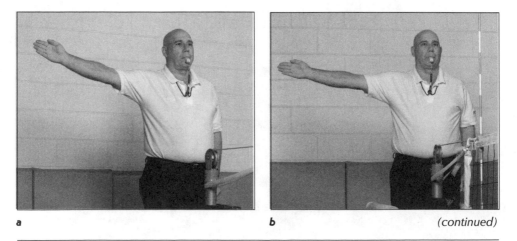

a　　　　　　　　　　　　　　　　b　　　　　　　　　　　　　　　　*(continued)*

Figure 3.7 Some signals commonly used by officials are *(a)* loss of rally or point, *(b)* ball in bounds.

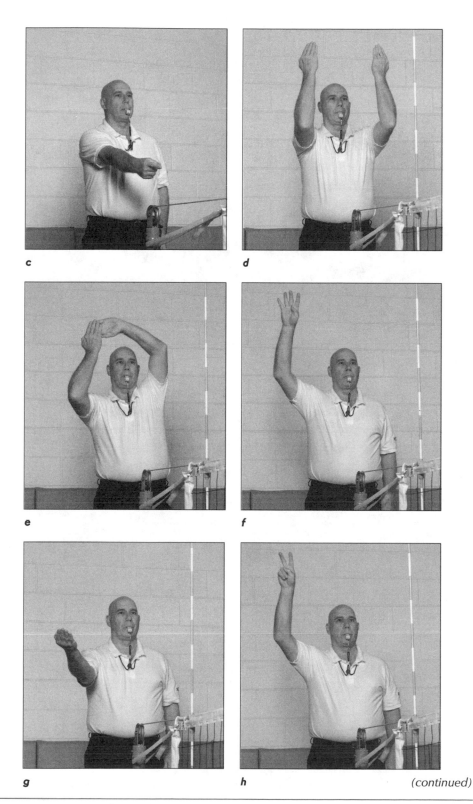

g　　　　　　　　　　　　　　　h　　　　　　　　　　　　　　　*(continued)*

Figure 3.7 *(c)* center line violation, *(d)* ball out, *(e)* ball out after contact with a player, *(f)* four hits, *(g)* held, thrown, lifted, or carried ball, *(h)* double hit.

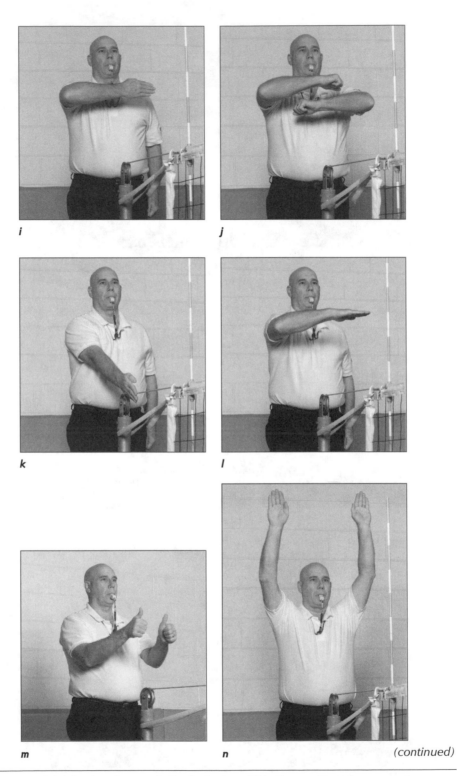

(continued)

Figure 3.7 *(i)* beckoning the serve, *(j)* substitution, *(k)* ball served into the net or player touching the net, *(l)* illegal attack or block over the net, *(m)* double fault or play over, *(n)* illegal block or screen.

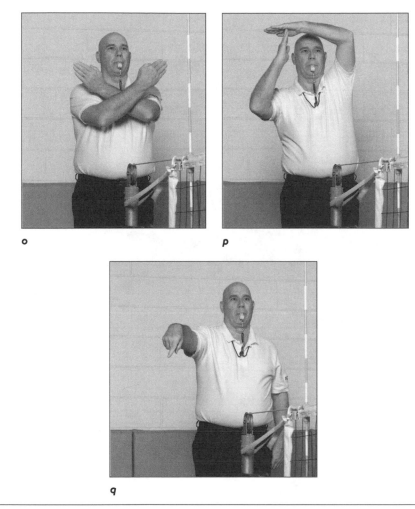

o

p

q

Figure 3.7 *(o)* end of game, *(p)* time-out, and *(q)* out of rotation or overlap.

4

Providing for Players' Safety

One of your players reacts quickly to the ball, diving to dig a spike hit toward the sideline. Incredibly, your player digs the ball to a teammate and saves the point. But just as you turn to praise the gutsy play, you see that the player is still down on the court. She is clutching her elbow and seems to be in pain. What do you do?

No coach wants to see players get hurt. But injury remains a reality of sport participation; consequently, you must be prepared to provide first aid when injuries occur and to protect yourself against unjustified lawsuits. Fortunately, coaches can institute many preventive measures to reduce the risk. In this chapter, we describe steps you can take to prevent injuries, first aid and emergency responses for when injuries occur, and your legal responsibilities as a coach.

Game Plan for Safety

You can't prevent all injuries from happening, but you can take preventive measures that give your players the best possible chance for injury-free participation. To help you create the safest possible environment for your players, we'll explore what you can do in these areas:

- Preseason physical examinations
- Physical conditioning
- Equipment and facilities inspection
- Player matchups
- Inherent risks
- Proper supervision and record keeping
- Environmental conditions

Preseason Physical Examination

We recommend that your players have a physical examination before participating in volleyball. The exam should address the most likely areas of medical concern and identify youngsters at high risk. We also suggest that you have players' parents or guardians sign a participation agreement form (this will be discussed in more detail later in this chapter) and an informed consent form to allow their children to be treated in case of an emergency. For a sample form, please see "Informed Consent Form" in appendix A on page 168.

Physical Conditioning

Players need to be in shape (or get in shape) to play the game at the level expected. They must have adequate cardiorespiratory fitness and muscular fitness.

Cardiorespiratory fitness involves the body's ability to use oxygen and fuels efficiently to power muscle contractions. As players get in better shape, their bodies are able to more efficiently deliver oxygen to fuel muscles and carry off carbon dioxides and other wastes. Volleyball requires lots of movement and the ability to make short bursts throughout a game. Youngsters who aren't as fit as their peers often overextend in trying to keep up, which can result in light-headedness, nausea, fatigue, and potential injury.

Try to remember that the players' goals are to participate, learn, and have fun. Therefore, you must keep the players active, attentive, and involved with every phase of practice. If you do, they will attain higher levels of cardiorespiratory fitness as the season progresses simply by taking part in practice. However, you should watch closely for signs of low cardiorespiratory fitness; don't let your players do much until they're fit. You might privately counsel youngsters who appear overly winded, suggesting that they train outside of practice (under proper supervision) to increase their fitness.

Muscular fitness encompasses strength, muscular endurance, power, speed, and flexibility. This type of fitness is affected by physical maturity, as well as strength training and other types of training. Your players will likely exhibit a relatively wide range of muscular fitness. Those who have greater muscular fitness will be able to run faster and hit the ball harder. They may also sustain fewer muscular injuries, and any injuries that do occur may tend to be minor. And in case of injury, recovery may be faster in those with higher levels of muscular fitness.

Two other components of fitness and injury prevention are the warm-up and the cool-down. Although young bodies are generally very limber, they can become tight through inactivity. The warm-up should address each muscle group and should elevate the heart rate in preparation for strenuous activity. Players should warm up for 5 to 10 minutes using a combination of light running, jumping, and active stretching (using movements specific to volleyball). As practice winds down, slow players' heart rates with an easy jog, walk, or volleyball movement drill. Then have the players stretch for 5 minutes to help prevent tight muscles before the next practice or game.

Coaching Tip

Younger players may not be aware of when they need a break for water and a short rest; therefore, you need to work regular breaks into your practice schedules. In addition, you should make sure that water is available at all times during the practice session. It is a good idea to have each player bring her own water bottle to practices and games. Each player has different hydration needs, and this will allow players to grab a drink when they need it, with the added benefit of reducing the need for long water breaks during the practice session.

Facilities and Equipment Inspection

Another way to prevent injuries is to regularly examine the court on which your players practice and play. Remove hazards, report conditions you cannot remedy, and request maintenance as necessary. For volleyball, this should include the floor and playing surface, the net and cables, and the standards and post pads. If unsafe conditions exist, you should either make adaptations to prevent risk to your players' safety or stop the practice or game until safe conditions have been restored. You can also prevent injuries by checking the quality and fit of uniforms, practice attire, and any protective equipment used by your players. Refer to the "Facilities and Equipment Checklist" in appendix A (page 166) to help guide you in verifying that facilities and equipment are safe.

Player Matchups

We recommend that you group teams in 2-year age increments if possible to help protect your players and to protect yourself from liability concerns. You'll encounter fewer mismatches in physical maturation with narrow age ranges. Even so, two 12-year-old children might differ by 60 pounds in weight, a foot in height, and 3 or 4 years in emotional and intellectual maturity. This presents dangers for the less mature. In your practices, you should match players against teammates of similar size and physical maturity whenever possible. Such an approach gives smaller, less mature youngsters a better chance to succeed and avoid injury while providing more mature players with a greater challenge. Closely supervise practices and games so that the more mature do not put the less mature at undue risk.

> **Coaching Tip**
> If your players vary widely in size, you should have players of similar size hit to each other during the warm-up. This will help prevent bigger players from hitting the ball too hard to smaller, less mature players who may have trouble digging hard hits.

Inherent Risks

You must warn players of the inherent risks involved in playing volleyball, because "failure to warn" is one of the most successful arguments in lawsuits against coaches. As a coach, you must be sure to thoroughly explain the inherent risks of volleyball, which include but are not limited to the following:

- Bumps
- Bruises
- Floor burns
- Jammed fingers or wrists
- Joint sprains (ankles, shoulder, elbow, or knee)
- Lower back and other muscle strains
- Scrapes or cuts
- Bloody nose

You can learn more about inherent risks by talking with your league administrators. In short, however, it is your responsibility to make sure that each player and each player's parents know, understand, and appreciate these inherent risks. The preseason parent-orientation meeting is a great opportunity to explain the risks of the sport to both parents and players. It is also a good time to have both the players and their parents sign a participation agreement form or waiver releasing you from liability should an injury occur. You should work with your league when creating these forms or waivers, and legal counsel should review them before presentation. These forms or waivers do not relieve you of responsibility for your players' well-being, but they are recommended by lawyers and may help you in the event of a lawsuit.

Proper Supervision and Record Keeping

To ensure players' safety, you must provide both general supervision and specific supervision. *General supervision* means that you are in the area of activity so that you can see and hear what is happening. You should be

- on the court and in position to supervise the players even before the formal practice begins,
- immediately accessible to the activity and able to oversee the entire activity,
- alert to conditions that may be dangerous to players and ready to take action to protect players,
- able to react immediately and appropriately to emergencies, and
- present on the court, in the facility, or in the parking lot until the last player has been picked up after the practice or game.

Specific supervision is the direct supervision of an activity at practice. For example, you should provide specific supervision when you teach new skills and should continue it until your players understand the requirements of the activity, the risks involved, and their own ability to perform in light of these risks. You must also provide specific supervision when you notice players breaking rules or a change in the condition of your players. As a general rule, the more dangerous the

Coaching Tip

Common sense tells us that it's easier to provide specific supervision to a smaller group of players, regardless of age. You should enlist the help of assistant coaches so that you can divide your team into smaller groups. This will help ensure that players can practice skills in a safe environment. The more adults who can help supervise, the better the players can learn and perform the skills of volleyball. In addition, smaller groups allow each coach to provide more direct feedback to players, and the players will get more contacts of the ball in the same length of time.

activity, the more specific the supervision required. This suggests that more specific supervision is required with younger and less experienced players.

As part of your supervision duty, you are expected to foresee potentially dangerous situations and to be positioned to help prevent them. This requires that you know volleyball well, especially the rules that are intended to provide for safety. Prohibit dangerous horseplay, and hold training sessions only under safe court and weather (for outdoor play) conditions. These specific supervisory activities, applied consistently, will make the play environment safer for your players and will help protect you from liability if a mishap occurs.

For further protection, keep written records of your season plans, practice plans, and players' injuries. Season and practice plans come in handy when you need evidence that players have been taught certain skills, whereas accurate, detailed injury report forms offer protection against unfounded lawsuits. Ask for these forms from your sponsoring organization (see page 169 in appendix A for a sample injury report form), and hold onto these records for several years so that an "old volleyball injury" of a former player doesn't come back to haunt you.

Environmental Conditions

Even though volleyball is a game that is typically played indoors, the versatility of the game allows it to be played outside as well. In addition, many players will practice on their own at outside courts, and many camps and youth practices are held outside because gym space is often limited or not available. Most health problems caused by environmental factors are related to excessive heat or cold, although you should also consider other environmental factors such as severe weather and air pollution. A little thought about the potential problems and a little effort to ensure adequate protection for your players will prevent most serious emergencies related to environmental conditions.

Heat

On hot, humid days the body has difficulty cooling itself. Because the air is already saturated with water vapor (humidity), sweat doesn't evaporate as easily. Therefore, body sweat is a less effective cooling agent, and the body retains extra heat. Hot, humid environments put players at risk of heat exhaustion and heatstroke (see more on these in "Serious Injuries" on pages 56-58). And if *you* think it's hot or humid, it's worse for the kids, not only because they're more active, but also because kids under the age of 12 have more difficulty regulating their body temperature than adults do. To provide for players' safety in hot or humid conditions, take the following preventive measures. Table 4.1 lists some warm-weather precautions for different temperatures.

- Monitor weather conditions and adjust training sessions accordingly.
- Acclimatize players to exercising in high heat and humidity. Athletes can

adjust to high heat and humidity in 7 to 10 days. During this period, hold practices at low to moderate activity levels and give the players fluid breaks at least every 20 minutes.

- Switch to light clothing. Players should wear light-colored shorts and T-shirts.

- Identify and monitor players who are prone to heat illness. This would include players who are overweight, heavily muscled, or out of shape and players who work excessively hard or have suffered previous heat illness. Closely monitor these players and give them fluid breaks at least every 15 to 20 minutes.

- Make sure players replace fluids lost through sweat. Encourage players to drink 17 to 20 ounces of fluid 2 to 3 hours before each practice or game, to drink 7 to 10 ounces every 20 minutes during practice and after practice, and to drink 16 to 24 ounces of fluid for every pound lost. Fluids such as water and sports drinks are preferable during games and practices (suggested intakes are based on NATA [National Athletic Trainers' Association] recommendations).

- Encourage players to replenish electrolytes, such as sodium (salt) and potassium, that are lost through sweat. The best way to replace these nutrients—as well as others such as carbohydrate (energy) and protein (muscle building)—is by eating a balanced diet. Experts say that additional salt intake in the diet may be helpful during the most intense training periods in the heat. Sports drinks may also be helpful in replacing electrolytes.

Coaching Tip

Encourage players to drink plenty of water before, during, and after practice. Water makes up 45 to 65 percent of a youngster's body weight, and even a small amount of water loss can cause severe consequences in the body's systems. It doesn't have to be hot and humid for players to become dehydrated, nor is thirst an accurate indicator. In fact, by the time players are aware of their thirst, they are long overdue for a drink. Therefore, you should be sure to schedule adequate water breaks and allow players to get a sip whenever they are not directly involved in a drill.

Table 4.1   Warm-Weather Precautions

Temperature (°F)	Humidity	Precautions
80-90	< 70%	Monitor players prone to heat illness
80-90	> 70%	5 min. rest after 30 min. of practice
90-100	< 70%	5 min. rest after 30 min. of practice
90-100	> 70%	Short practices in evenings or early morning

Cold

When a person is exposed to cold weather, the body temperature starts to drop below normal. To counteract this, the body shivers to create heat and reduces blood flow to the extremities to conserve heat in the core of the body. But no matter how effective the body's natural heating mechanism is, the body will better withstand cold temperatures if it is prepared to handle them. To reduce the risk of cold-related illnesses, make sure players wear appropriate protective clothing, and keep the players active to maintain body heat. Also monitor the windchill factor because it can drastically affect the severity of players' responses to the weather. The windchill factor index is shown in figure 4.1.

					Temperature (°F)				
	0	5	10	15	20	25	30	35	40
	Flesh may freeze within one minute								
40	-55	-45	-35	-30	-20	-15	-5	0	10
35	-50	-40	-35	-30	-20	-10	-5	5	10
30	-50	-40	-30	-25	-20	-10	0	5	10
25	-45	-35	-30	-20	-15	-5	0	10	15
20	-35	-30	-25	-15	-10	0	5	10	20
15	-30	-25	-20	-10	-5	0	10	15	25
10	-20	-15	-10	0	5	10	15	20	30
5	-5	0	5	10	15	20	25	30	35

Wind speed (mph)

Windchill temperature (°F)

Figure 4.1   Windchill factor index.

Severe Weather

Severe weather refers to a host of potential dangers, including lightning storms, tornadoes, hail, and heavy rains. When playing volleyball outside, lightning is of special concern because it can come up quickly and can cause great harm or even kill. For each 5-second count from the flash of lightning to the bang of thunder, lightning is one mile away. A flash-bang of 10 seconds means lightning is two miles away; a flash-bang of 15 seconds indicates lightning is three miles away. A practice or competition should be stopped for the day if lightning is six miles away or closer (30 seconds or less from flash to bang). In addition to these suggestions, your school, league, or state association may also have rules that you will want to consider in severe weather.

Safe places to take cover when lightning strikes include fully enclosed metal vehicles with the windows up, enclosed buildings, and low ground (under cover of bushes, if possible). It's not safe to be near metal objects such as volleyball standards, flag poles, fences, light poles, and metal bleachers. Also avoid trees, water, and open fields.

You should cancel practice when under either a tornado watch or warning. If you are practicing or competing when a tornado is nearby, you should get inside a building if possible. If you cannot get into a building, lie in a ditch or other low-lying area or crouch near a strong building, using your arms to protect your head and neck.

The keys to handling severe weather are caution and prudence. Don't try to get that last 10 minutes of practice in if lightning is on the horizon. Don't continue to play in heavy rain. Many storms can strike both quickly and ferociously. Respect the weather and play it safe.

Air Pollution

Poor air quality and smog can present real dangers to your players. Both short- and long-term lung damage are possible from participating in unsafe air. Although it's true that participating in clean air is not possible in many areas, restricting activity is recommended when the air quality ratings are lower than moderate or when there is a smog alert. Your local health department or air quality control board can inform you of the air quality ratings for your area and when restricting activities is recommended.

Responding to Players' Injuries

No matter how good and thorough your prevention program is, injuries most likely will occur. When injury does strike, chances are you will be the one in charge. The severity and nature of the injury will determine how actively involved you'll be in treating it. But regardless of how seriously a player is hurt, it is your responsibility to know what steps to take. Therefore, you must be prepared to take appropriate action and provide basic emergency care when an injury occurs.

Being Prepared

Being prepared to provide basic emergency care involves many things, including being trained in cardiopulmonary resuscitation (CPR) and first aid, having a first aid kit on hand, and having an emergency plan.

CPR and First Aid Training

We recommend that all coaches receive CPR and first aid training from a nationally recognized organization such as the National Safety Council, the American Heart Association, the American Red Cross, or the American Sport Education Program (ASEP). You should be certified based on a practical test and a written test of knowledge. CPR training should include pediatric and adult basic life support and obstructed airway procedures.

First Aid Kit

A well-stocked first aid kit should include the following:

- Antibacterial soap or wipes
- Arm sling
- Athletic tape—one and a half inches wide
- Bandage scissors
- Bandage strips—assorted sizes
- Blood spill kit
- Cell phone
- Contact lens case
- Cotton swabs
- Elastic wraps—three inches, four inches, and six inches
- Emergency blanket
- Examination gloves—latex free
- Eye patch
- Foam rubber—one-eighth inch, one-fourth inch, and one-half inch
- Insect sting kit
- List of emergency phone numbers
- Mirror
- Moleskin
- Nail clippers
- Oral thermometer (to determine if a player has a fever caused by illness)
- Penlight
- Petroleum jelly
- Plastic bags for crushed ice
- Prewrap (underwrap for tape)
- Rescue breathing or CPR face mask
- Safety glasses (for first aiders)
- Safety pins
- Saline solution for eyes
- Sterile gauze pads—three-inch and four-inch squares (preferably nonstick)
- Sterile gauze rolls
- Sunscreen—sun protection factor (SPF) 30 or greater

- Tape adherent and tape remover
- Tongue depressors
- Tooth saver kit
- Triangular bandages
- Tweezers

Adapted, by permission, from M. Flegel, 2004, *Sport first aid*, 3rd ed. (Champaign, IL: Human Kinetics), 20.

Emergency Plan

An emergency plan is the final step in being prepared to take appropriate action for severe or serious injuries. The plan calls for three steps:

1. *Evaluate the injured player.*

   Use your CPR and first aid training to guide you. Be sure to keep these certifications up-to-date. Practice your skills frequently to keep them fresh and ready to use if and when you need them.

2. *Call the appropriate medical personnel.*

   If possible, delegate the responsibility of seeking medical help to another calm and responsible adult who attends all practices and games. Write out a list of emergency phone numbers and keep it with you at practices and games. Include the following phone numbers:

   - Rescue unit
   - Hospital
   - Physician
   - Police
   - Fire department

   Take each player's emergency information to every practice and game (see "Emergency Information Card" in appendix A on page 170). This information includes the person to contact in case of an emergency, what types of medications the player is using, what types of drugs the player is allergic to, and so on.

   Give an emergency response card (see "Emergency Response Card" in appendix A on page 171) to the contact person calling for emergency assistance. Having this information ready should help the contact person remain calm. Following the incident, you must also complete an injury report form (see page 169 in appendix A) and keep it on file for any injury that occurs.

3. *Provide first aid.*

   If medical personnel are not on hand at the time of the injury, you should provide first aid care to the extent of your qualifications. Again, although your CPR and first aid training will guide you, you must remember the following:

- Do not move the injured player if the injury is to the head, neck, or back; if a large joint (ankle, knee, elbow, shoulder) is dislocated; or if the pelvis, a rib, or an arm or leg is fractured.

- Calm the injured player and keep others away from her as much as possible; her teammates will also likely be anxious, so assign someone to gather them away from the injured player and assure them that their teammate will be okay.

- Evaluate whether the player's breathing has stopped or is irregular, and if necessary, clear the airway with your fingers.

- Administer CPR as directed in the CPR certification course recommended by your school, league, or state association.

- Remain with the player until medical personnel arrive.

Emergency Steps

You must have a clear, well-rehearsed emergency action plan. You want to be sure you are prepared in case of an emergency because every second counts. Your emergency plan should follow this sequence:

1. Check the player's level of consciousness.

2. Send a contact person to call the appropriate medical personnel and to call the player's parents if they are not present.

3. Send someone to wait for the rescue team and direct them to the injured player.

4. Assess the injury.

5. Administer first aid.

6. Assist emergency medical personnel in preparing the player for transportation to a medical facility.

7. Appoint someone to go with the player if the parents are not available. This person should be responsible, calm, and familiar with the player. Assistant coaches or parents are best for this job.

8. Complete an injury report form while the incident is fresh in your mind (see page 169 in appendix A).

Taking Appropriate Action

Proper CPR and first aid training, a well-stocked first aid kit, and an emergency plan help prepare you to take appropriate action when an injury occurs. In the previous section, we mentioned the importance of providing first aid to the extent of your qualifications. Don't "play doctor" with injuries; sort out minor injuries that you can treat from those that need medical attention. Now let's look at taking the appropriate action for minor injuries and more serious injuries.

Minor Injuries

Although no injury seems minor to the person experiencing it, most injuries are neither life threatening nor severe enough to restrict participation. When these injuries occur, you can take an active role in their initial treatment.

Scrapes and Cuts   When one of your players has an open wound, the first thing you should do is put on a pair of disposable latex-free examination gloves or some other effective blood barrier. Then follow these four steps:

> **Coaching Tip**
>
> You shouldn't let a fear of acquired immune deficiency syndrome (AIDS) and other communicable diseases stop you from helping a player. You are only at risk if you allow contaminated blood to come in contact with an open wound on your body, so the examination gloves that you wear will protect you from AIDS if one of your players carries this disease. Check with your sport director, your league, or the Centers for Disease Control and Prevention (CDC) for more information about protecting yourself and your participants from AIDS.

1. Stop the bleeding by applying direct pressure with a clean dressing to the wound and elevating it. The player may be able to apply this pressure while you put on your gloves. Do not remove the dressing if it becomes soaked with blood. Instead, place an additional dressing on top of the one already in place. If bleeding continues, elevate the injured area above the heart and maintain pressure.

2. Cleanse the wound thoroughly once the bleeding is controlled. A good rinsing with a forceful stream of water, and perhaps light scrubbing with soap, will help prevent infection.

3. Protect the wound with sterile gauze or a bandage strip. If rules allow the player to continue to participate, apply protective padding over the injured area.

4. Remove and dispose of gloves carefully to prevent you or anyone else from coming into contact with blood.

For bloody noses not associated with serious facial injury, have the player sit and lean slightly forward. Then pinch the player's nostrils shut. If the bleeding continues after several minutes, or if the player has a history of nosebleeds, seek medical assistance.

Strains and Sprains   The physical demands of playing volleyball often result in injury to the muscles or tendons (strains) or to the ligaments (sprains). When your players suffer minor strains or sprains, you should immediately apply the PRICE method of injury care:

P Protect the player and the injured body part from further danger or trauma.

R Rest the injured area to avoid further damage and foster healing.

I Ice the area to reduce swelling and pain.

C Compress the area by securing an ice bag in place with an elastic wrap.

E Elevate the injury above heart level to keep the blood from pooling in the area.

Bumps and Bruises   Inevitably, volleyball players make contact with each other, the ball, the net or standards, and the ground. If the force applied to a body part at impact is great enough, a bump or bruise will result. Many players continue playing with such sore spots, but if the bump or bruise is large and painful, you should take appropriate action. Again, use the PRICE method for injury care and monitor the injury. If swelling, discoloration, and pain have lessened, the player may resume participation with protective padding; if not, the player should be examined by a physician.

Serious Injuries

Head, neck, and back injuries; fractures; and injuries that cause a player to lose consciousness are among a class of injuries that you cannot and should not try to treat yourself. In these cases, you should follow the emergency plan outlined on page 53. We do want to examine more closely, however, your role in preventing and attending to heat cramps, heat exhaustion, and heatstroke. Additionally, please refer to figure 4.2 for an illustrative example of the signs and symptoms associated with heat exhaustion and heatstroke.

Heat Cramps   Tough practices combined with heat stress and substantial fluid loss from sweating can provoke muscle cramps commonly known as *heat cramps*. Cramping is most common when the weather is hot. Depending

Heat exhaustion   **Heatstroke**

Dizziness ———————————————— Dizziness

Headache ——————————————— Headache

Fatigue ——————————— Disoriented, combative,
or unconscious

Dehydration —————————— Dehydration

Profuse sweating ——————— Severely increased
body temperature

Mildly increased
body temperature ——————— Hot and wet
or dry skin

Nausea or
vomiting ———————— Nausea or
vomiting

Diarrhea ——————— Diarrhea

Muscle cramps ———————

Figure 4.2 Signs and symptoms of heat exhaustion and heatstroke.

on your location, it may be hot early in the season, which can be problematic because players may be less conditioned and less adapted to heat. In other locations, it may be hot later in the season, when players are better conditioned but still not used to playing in high temperatures. A cramp, a severe tightening of the muscle, can drop players and prevent continued play. Dehydration, electrolyte loss, and fatigue are the contributing factors. The immediate treatment is to have the player cool off, replace fluids lost through activity, and slowly stretch the contracted muscle. The player may return to play later that same day or the next day provided the cramp doesn't cause a muscle strain.

Heat Exhaustion   Heat exhaustion is a shocklike condition caused by strenuous activity combined with heat stress. This, in addition to dehydration and electrolyte depletion, does not allow the body to keep up. Symptoms include fatigue, dizziness, headache, nausea, vomiting, diarrhea, and muscle cramps. Difficulty continuing activity, profuse sweating, and mildly increased body temperature are key signs of heat exhaustion.

A player suffering from heat exhaustion should rest in a cool, shaded, or air-conditioned area with her legs propped above heart level; remove excess clothing and equipment; drink cool fluids, particularly those containing electrolytes (if not nauseated); and apply ice to the neck, back, or abdomen to help cool the body. If you believe a player is suffering from heat exhaustion, seek medical attention. Under no conditions should the player return to activity that day. In this situation, we recommend that the player not return to activity until she has a written release from a physician.

Heatstroke   Heatstroke is a life-threatening condition in which the body stops sweating and body temperature rises dangerously high. It results from the continuation of strenuous activity in extreme temperatures. Heatstroke occurs when dehydration and electrolyte depletion cause a malfunction in the body's temperature control center in the brain. Symptoms include fatigue, dizziness, confusion, irritability, hysteria, nausea, vomiting, diarrhea, and the feeling of being extremely hot. Signs include hot and wet or dry skin; rapid pulse and rapid breathing; and possible seizures, unconsciousness, or respiratory or cardiac arrest.

If you suspect that a player is suffering from heatstroke, send for emergency medical assistance immediately, and cool the player as quickly as possible. Remove excess clothing and equipment, and cool the player's body with cool, wet towels; by pouring cool water over the player; or by placing the player in a cold bath. Apply ice packs to the armpits, neck, back, abdomen, and between the legs. If the player is conscious, give her cool fluids to drink. If the player is unconscious or falls unconscious, place the player on her side to allow fluids and vomit to drain from the mouth. A player who has suffered heatstroke may not return to the team until she has a written release from a physician.

Protecting Yourself

When one of your players is injured, naturally your first concern is the player's well-being. Your feelings for youngsters, after all, are what made you decide to coach. Unfortunately, you must also consider something else: Can you be held liable for the injury?

From a legal standpoint, a coach must fulfill nine duties. We've discussed all but planning in this chapter (planning is discussed in chapters 5 and 10). The following is a summary of your legal duties:

1. Provide a safe environment.
2. Properly plan the activity.
3. Provide adequate and proper equipment.
4. Match players appropriately.
5. Warn of inherent risks in the sport.

6. Supervise the activity closely.

7. Evaluate players for injury or incapacitation.

8. Know emergency procedures, CPR, and first aid.

9. Keep adequate records.

In addition to fulfilling these nine legal duties, you should check your organization's insurance coverage and your own insurance coverage to make sure these policies will properly protect you from liability.

5

Making Practices Fun and Practical

In the past, we have placed too much emphasis on the learning of individual skills and not enough on learning how to play skillfully—that is, how to integrate and use those skills in competition. The games approach, in contrast to the traditional approach, emphasizes learning what to do first, then how to do it. Moreover, the games approach lets kids discover what to do in the game, not by your telling them, but by their experiencing it. It is a guided discovery method of teaching that empowers your kids to solve the problems that arise in the game, which is a large part of the fun in learning.

On the surface, it would seem to make sense to introduce volleyball using the traditional approach—by first teaching each basic skill of the sport and then the tactics of the game—but this approach has been shown to have disadvantages. First, it teaches the skills of the sport out of the context of the game. Kids may learn to pass, set, spike, and dig, but they find it difficult to use these skills in the real game. This is because they do not yet understand the basic tactical skills of volleyball and do not appreciate how best to use their newfound technical skills in actual competition. Second, learning individual skills by doing repetitive drills outside of the context of the game is downright boring. The single biggest turnoff in sports is overorganized instruction that deprives kids of their intrinsic desire to play the game.

The games approach is taught using a four-step process. These steps are as follows:

1. Play a modified game.
2. Help the players discover what they need to do to play the game successfully.
3. Teach the skills of the game.
4. Practice the skills in another game.

Step 1: Play a Modified Game

It's the first day of practice; some of the kids are eager to get started, while others are obviously apprehensive. Some have rarely served a ball, most don't know the rules, and few know the positions in volleyball. What do you do?

If you used the traditional approach, you would start with a quick warm-up activity, then line the players up for a simple passing drill and go from there. With the games approach, however, you begin by playing a modified game that is developmentally appropriate for the level of the players and also designed to focus on learning a specific part of the game (e.g., passing skills).

Modifying the game emphasizes a limited number of situations in the game. This is one way you "guide" your players to discover certain tactics in the game. For example, you could have your players play a 3v3 game on a smaller court where one player is designated as the passer, one as the setter, and one as the hitter. The objective of the game is to make passes to set up an attack on the third contact. Playing the game this way forces players to think about what they have to do to set up an effective attack—without the added pressure of a large court or additional player responsibilities when there are more players on the court.

Activities Checklist

When developing activities for your youth volleyball program, here are a few questions that you should ask yourself:

- Are the activities fun?
- Are the activities organized?
- Are all players involved in the activities?
- Do the activities require the players to use creativity and decision making?
- Are all the available spaces used appropriately?
- Is the coach's feedback appropriate?
- Are there direct implications for how the game is actually played?

Step 2: Help Players Understand the Game

As your players are playing a modified game, you should look for the right spot to "freeze" the action, step in, and ask questions about errors that you're seeing. When you do this, you help the players better understand the objective of the game, what they must do to achieve that objective, and also what skills they must use to achieve that objective.

Asking the right questions is a very important part of your teaching. Essentially, you'll be asking your players—often literally—"What do you need to do to succeed in this situation?" Sometimes players simply need to have more time playing the game, or you may need to modify the game further so that it is even easier for them to discover what they need to do. It may take more patience and work on your part, but it's a powerful way for kids to learn. For example, assume your players are playing a game in which the objective is to make good forearm passes, but they are having trouble doing so. Interrupt the action and ask the following questions:

- What are you supposed to do in this game?
- What do you have to do to get the ball to the setter?
- Who should call and pass a ball that is falling in the right-back area of the court?
- Who should call and pass the ball if it is hit between the left-back and right-back players?

Coaching Tip

If your players have trouble understanding what to do, you can phrase your questions to let the players choose between one option or another. For example, if you ask them, "What's the best way to get the ball to the setter if it is high in your area of the court?" and get an answer such as "Pass it," then ask, "Should it be an overhead or a forearm pass?"

At first, asking the right questions might seem difficult because your players have little or no experience with the game. And, if you've learned sport through the traditional approach, you'll be tempted to tell your players how to play the game rather than "wasting time" asking questions. When using the games approach, however, you must resist this powerful temptation to tell your players what to do. You must ask them instead.

Through modified games and skillful questioning on your part, your players should come to the realization on their own that accurate passing skills and tactical awareness are essential to their success in being able to run an effective attack. Just as important, rather than telling them what the critical skills are, you led them to this discovery, which is a crucial part of the games approach.

Step 3: Teach the Skills of the Game

Only when your players recognize the skills they need to be successful in the game do you want to teach these specific skills through focused activities in a specific game situation. This is when you can use a more traditional approach to teaching sport skills, the "IDEA" approach, which we will describe in chapter 6. This type of teaching breaks down the skills of the game. It should be implemented early in the season so that players can begin attaining skill, which will make games more fun.

Step 4: Practice the Skills in Another Game

As a coach, you want your players to experience success as they're learning skills, and the best way for them to experience this success early on is for you to create an advantage for the players. Once the players have practiced the skill, as outlined in step 3, you can then put them in another game situation—this time with a defensive advantage. For example, instead of having just one passer (e.g., the left-back player) on the court, you can add the additional passer in the right-back and possibly also in the center-back positions. The idea is that this makes it more likely that, for instance, with more passers on the court, your players will be able to successfully pass the ball and get the ball to the setter for a set and then the attack.

We recommend first using a normal game situation (that is, the typical number of players for the age group) and then introducing games where one side has an advantage. This sequence enables you to first introduce your players to a situation similar to what they will experience in competition, and to let them discover the challenges they face in performing the necessary skill. Then you teach them the skill, have them practice it, and put them back in another game—this time using an advantage to give them a greater chance of experiencing success.

As players improve their skills, however, you may not need to provide an advantage. Having extra players will eventually become too easy and won't challenge your players to hone their skills. When this time comes, you can lessen the advantage, or you may even decide that they're ready to practice the skill as they would use it in regular competition. The key is to set up gamelike situations where your players experience success yet are challenged in doing so. This will take careful monitoring on your part, but having kids play altered games as they are learning skills is a very effective way of helping them learn and improve.

And that's the games approach. Your players will get to play more in practice, and once they learn how the skills fit into their performance and enjoyment of the game, they'll be more motivated to work on those skills, which will help them to be successful.

6

Teaching and Shaping Skills

Coaching volleyball is about teaching kids how to play the game by teaching them skills, fitness, and values. It's also about coaching players before, during, and after games. Teaching and coaching are closely related, but there are important differences. In this chapter, we focus on principles of teaching, especially on teaching technical and tactical skills. But these principles apply to teaching values and fitness concepts as well. Armed with these principles, you will be able to design effective and efficient practices and will understand how to deal with misbehavior. Then you will be able to teach the skills and plays necessary to be successful in volleyball (which are outlined in chapters 7 and 8).

Teaching Volleyball Skills

Many people believe that the only qualification needed to teach a skill is to have performed it. Although it's helpful to have performed it, teaching it successfully requires much more than that. And even if you haven't performed the skill before, you can still learn to teach successfully with the useful acronym IDEA:

I   Introduce the skill.

D   Demonstrate the skill.

E   Explain the skill.

A   Attend to players practicing the skill.

Introduce the Skill

Players, especially those who are young and inexperienced, need to know what skill they are learning and why they are learning it. You should therefore use the following three steps every time you introduce a skill to your players:

1. Get your players' attention.
2. Name the skill.
3. Explain the importance of the skill.

Get Your Players' Attention

Because youngsters are easily distracted, you should do something to get their attention. Some coaches use interesting news items or stories. Others use jokes. And still others simply project enthusiasm to get their players to listen. Whatever method you use, speak slightly above your normal volume and look your players in the eye when you speak.

Also, position players so they can see and hear you. Arrange the players in two or three evenly spaced rows, facing you. (Make sure they aren't looking into the sun, through windows, or at a distracting activity going on behind you.) Then ask whether all of them can see you before you begin to speak.

Name the Skill

More than one common name may exist for the skill you are introducing, but you should decide as a staff before the start of the season which one you'll use (and then stick with it). This will help prevent confusion and enhance communication among your players. When you introduce the new skill, call it by name several times so that the players automatically correlate the name with the skill in later discussions.

> **Coaching Tip**
> You should write out in detail each skill you will teach. This will help clarify what you will say and how you will demonstrate and teach each skill to your players. Try to limit the cues you will give the players to no more than four cues consisting of no more than four words each. This will help you keep your explanations short and to the point, and players won't be confused with too much information at once.

Explain the Importance of the Skill

As Rainer Martens, the founder of the American Sport Education Program (ASEP), has said, "The most difficult aspect of coaching is this: Coaches must learn to let athletes learn. Sport skills should be taught so they have meaning to the child, not just meaning to the coach." Although the importance of a skill may be apparent to you, your players may be less able to see how the skill will help them become better volleyball players. Offer them a reason for learning the skill, and describe how the skill relates to more advanced skills and to playing the game itself.

Demonstrate the Skill

The demonstration step is the most important part of teaching sport skills to players who may never have done anything closely resembling the skill. They need a picture, not just words, so they can see how the skill is performed. Think in terms of the favorite kindergarten activity of "Show and Tell." If you are unable to perform the skill correctly, ask an assistant coach, one of your players, or someone more skilled to perform the demonstration. Keep in mind that the most effective models are players who are close to your players' own age and skill level. This helps promote the idea that "If she can do it, I can too." Sometimes photos or videos can help provide the proper "picture" a player needs of the skill.

These tips will help make your demonstrations more effective:

- Use correct form.
- Demonstrate the skill several times, first without the ball, then with the ball.
- Slow the action, if possible, during one or two performances so players can see every movement involved in the skill.
- Perform the skill at different angles so your players can get a full perspective of it.
- Demonstrate the skill with both sides of the body, especially if you have left-handed players on your team.

Explain the Skill

Players learn more effectively when they're given a brief explanation of the skill along with the demonstration. You should use simple terms and, if possible, relate the skill to previously learned skills. Ask your players whether they understand your description. A good technique is to ask the team to repeat your explanation. Ask questions such as "What are you going to do first?" and "Then what?" If players look confused or uncertain, you should repeat your explanation and demonstration. If possible, use different words so your players get a chance to try to understand the skill from a different perspective.

Complex skills are often better understood when they are explained in more manageable parts. For instance, if you want to teach your players how to approach and hit a spike, you might take the following steps:

1. Show them a correct performance of the entire skill, without and with the ball, and explain its function in volleyball.
2. Break down the skill and point out its component parts to your players (e.g., approach, jump, and swing).
3. Have players perform each of the component skills you have already taught them, such as assuming a ready position and moving to the set.
4. After players have demonstrated their ability to perform the separate parts of the skill in sequence, reexplain and demonstrate the entire skill.
5. Have players practice the skill in gamelike conditions.

Young players have short attention spans, and a long demonstration or explanation of a skill may cause them to lose focus. Therefore, you should spend no more than two to three minutes altogether on the introduction, demonstration, and explanation phases. Then involve the players in drills or games that call on them to perform the skill as soon as possible.

How to Properly Run Your Drills

Before running a drill that teaches technique, you should do the following:

- Name the drill.
- Explain the skill or skills to be practiced.
- Position the players correctly and show the proper rotation through the drill, including how and when balls are to be retrieved and entered into the drill.
- Explain what the drill will accomplish, including the goal and scoring system for the drill.
- Identify the command that will start the drill.
- Identify the command that will end the drill, such as a whistle, or the scoring system that will cue the rotation or the end of the drill.

Once the drill has been introduced and repeated a few times in this manner, you will find that merely calling out the name of the drill is sufficient; your players will automatically line up in the proper position to run the drill and practice the skill.

Attend to Players Practicing the Skill

If the skill you selected was within your players' capabilities and you have done an effective job of introducing, demonstrating, and explaining it, your players should be ready to attempt the skill within a drill or game. Some players, especially those in younger age groups, may need to be physically guided through the movements during their first few attempts. Walking unsure players through the skill in this way will help them gain confidence to perform the skill on their own.

Your teaching duties, though, don't end when all your players have demonstrated that they understand how to perform a skill. In fact, your teaching role is just beginning as you help your players improve their skills. A significant part of your teaching consists of closely observing the hit-and-miss trial performances of your players. You will shape players' skills by detecting errors and correcting them using positive feedback. Keep in mind that your positive feedback will have a great influence on your players' motivation to practice and improve their performances.

Remember, too, that some players may need individual instruction. So set aside a time before, during, or after practice to give individual help. Individual players may also be pulled out of a drill for individual correction (tutoring), then inserted back into the drill. This way, the drill doesn't need to be stopped for the majority of players when only one or two need individual help.

Helping Players Improve Skills

After you have successfully taught your players the fundamentals of a skill, your focus will be on helping them improve the skill. Players learn skills and improve on them at different rates, so don't get frustrated if progress seems slow. Instead, help them improve by shaping their skills and detecting and correcting frequently occurring errors.

Shaping Players' Skills

One of your principal teaching duties is to reward positive effort or behavior—in terms of successful skill execution—when you see it. Catch them doing it right and be specific about what you observed. A player makes a good pass in practice, and you immediately say, "Good pass! Way to use your fingers rather than your palms on that set—it was right on target for the hitter!" This, plus a smile and a "thumbs-up" gesture, goes a long way toward reinforcing that technique in that player. However, sometimes you may have a long dry spell before you see correct techniques to reinforce. It's difficult to reward players when they don't execute skills correctly. How can you shape their skills if this is the case?

Shaping skills takes practice on your players' part and patience on yours. Expect your players to make errors. Telling the player who made the great pass that she did a good job doesn't ensure that she'll have the same success next time. Seeing inconsistency in your players' technique can be frustrating. It's even more challenging to stay positive when your players repeatedly perform a skill incorrectly or have a lack of enthusiasm for learning. It can certainly be frustrating to see players who seemingly don't heed your advice and continue to make the same mistakes.

Although it is normal to get frustrated sometimes when teaching skills, part of successful coaching is controlling this frustration. Instead of getting upset, use these six guidelines for shaping skills:

1. *Think small initially.*

   Reward the first signs of behavior that approximate what you want. Then reward closer and closer approximations of the desired behavior. In short, use your reward power to shape the behavior you seek.

2. *Break skills into small steps.*

   For instance, in learning the overhand serve, one of your players does well with her swing, but her toss is inconsistent. Reinforce the correct technique of her swing, and teach her how to make more consistent tosses. Once she masters this, you can focus on getting her to complete the skill by serving to certain areas of the court.

3. *Develop one component of a skill at a time.*

   Don't try to shape two or more components of a skill at once. Instead, limit your feedback to just one aspect of the skill until that aspect is mastered, then address the others one at a time. For example, when receiving a serve, players must first move to the correct location, assume the correct body position, and execute the pass. Players should focus first on one aspect (moving to the correct location), then on another (assuming the correct body position), and then another (executing the pass). Players who have problems mastering a skill often do so because they're trying to improve two or more components at once. You should help these players to isolate a single component by targeting your feedback to that specific component.

4. *Use reinforcement only occasionally, for the best examples.*

   By focusing only on the best examples, you will help players continue to improve once they've mastered the basics. Using occasional reinforcement during practice allows players to have more contact time with the ball rather than having to constantly stop and listen to the coach. Stop the entire group only if the whole group is making the same sort of error and all players need to hear the correction in order to perform better. Volleyball skills are best learned through a lot of repetition, such as in gamelike drills, and the coach needs to make the best use of team practice time by allowing the players to have as much playing time as possible.

5. *Relax your reward standards.*

   As players focus on mastering a new skill or attempt to integrate it with other skills, their old, well-learned skills may temporarily degenerate, and you may need to relax your expectations. For example, a player has learned a floater serve using a basic overhand serving motion and is now learning how to modify that technique to develop a topspin serve. While learning to adjust the toss and contact position and getting the timing down on the topspin serve, the player's execution of the floater serve may be poor. A similar degeneration of skills may occur during growth spurts while the coordination of muscles, tendons, and ligaments catches up to the growth of bones.

6. *Go back to the basics.*

   If, however, a well-learned skill degenerates for long, you may need to restore it by going back to the basics. If necessary, players should practice the skill using an activity that involves less pressure from opponents so that they can relearn the skill (for example, a server can practice with only a target on the floor to focus on, adding a passer only when she's comfortable with her serve again).

Coaching Tip

For older age groups or players with advanced skills, coaches can ask players to "self-coach." With the proper guidance (including guiding questions from the coach) and a positive team environment, young players can think about how they perform a skill and how they might be able to perform it better. Self-coaching is best done at practice, where a player can experiment with learning new skills.

Detecting and Correcting Errors

Good coaches recognize that players make two types of errors: learning errors and performance errors. Learning errors are ones that occur because players don't know how to perform a skill; that is, they have not yet developed the correct motor pattern in the brain to perform a particular skill. Performance errors are made not because players don't know how to execute the skill, but because they have made a mistake in executing what they do know or have made errors in anticipation, reading, judgment, or timing. There is no easy way to know whether a player is making learning or performance errors; part of the art of coaching is being able to sort out which type of error each mistake is.

The process of helping your players correct errors begins with you observing and evaluating their performances to determine if the mistakes are learning or performance errors. You should carefully watch your players to see if they routinely make the errors in both practice and game settings, or if the errors tend to occur only in game settings. If the latter is the case, then your players are making performance errors. For performance errors, you need to look for the reasons your players are not performing as well as they know how; perhaps they are nervous, or maybe they get distracted by the game setting. If you suspect that the mistakes are learning errors, you can ask the players to perform the same skill without the ball. If they cannot perform the skill without the ball, you need to help them learn the skill, which is the focus of this section. If the players can perform the skill without the ball, then chances are their mistakes are performance errors in anticipation, reading, judgment, or timing.

When correcting learning errors, there is no substitute for knowledge of the skills. The better you understand a skill—not only how it is performed correctly but also what causes learning errors—the more helpful you will be in correcting your players' mistakes.

One of the most common coaching mistakes is to provide inaccurate feedback and advice on how to correct errors. Don't rush into error correction; wrong feedback or poor advice will hurt the learning process more than no feedback or advice at all. If you are uncertain about the cause of the problem or how to correct it, you should continue to observe and analyze until you are more sure. As a rule, you should see the error repeated several times before attempting to correct it. This is often called *coaching on the averages* or *summary feedback*.

Correct One Error at a Time

Suppose Megan, one of your attackers, is having trouble with her spiking. She does most things well, but you notice that she's swinging her arms forward and up rather late as she approaches the ball, and she's contacting the ball behind her hitting shoulder, thus causing her spikes to go high. What do you do?

First, decide which error to correct first, because players learn more effectively when they attempt to correct one error at a time. Determine whether each error is one of technique or one of performance (anticipation, reading, judgment, or timing) and whether one error is causing the other; if so, have the player correct that error first, because it may eliminate the other error. In Megan's case, raising her arms late may be causing her to contact the ball too low. But if the ball is behind her hitting shoulder, the first problem might be that she is running in too early to jump, or she is overrunning the set ball; therefore, you should correct her approach timing or jump positioning first, and then help her with the late arm motion. Megan needs to work on waiting a bit longer after the ball has been set to begin her approach or stopping in a position farther off the net to jump. Once she improves her ability to judge the set and get in proper position to jump, then she should work on her swing so that it is higher and faster and contacts the ball sooner. Note that improvement in the first area may even motivate her to correct the other errors.

Use Positive Feedback to Correct Errors

The positive approach to correcting errors includes emphasizing what to do instead of what not to do. Use compliments, praise, rewards, and encouragement to correct errors. Acknowledge correct performance as well as efforts to improve. By using positive feedback, you can help your players feel good about themselves and promote a strong desire to achieve.

When you're working with one player at a time, the positive approach to correcting errors includes four steps:

1. *Praise effort and correct performance.*

   Praise the player for effort in trying to perform a skill correctly and for performing any parts of it correctly. Praise the player immediately after she performs the skill, if possible. Keep the praise simple, but specific: "Good try" should be expanded to include "Good high elbow on that swing." "Way to hustle" may be expanded to "Way to hustle to get behind that ball on your pass." "Good form" can be expanded to "Good form on that forearm pass platform." "That's the way to follow through" can be rephrased to say, "That's the way to follow through to the target." Any positive but nonspecific comment such as "Good job" should be followed up with the specific portion of the skill you are commenting on—for example, "Good job, you used your three-step approach!" You can also use nonverbal feedback, such as smiling, clapping your hands, or any facial or body expression that shows approval.

Make sure you're sincere with your praise. Don't indicate that a player's effort was good when it wasn't. Usually a player knows when she has made a sincere effort to perform the skill correctly and perceives undeserved praise for what it is—untruthful feedback to make her feel good. Likewise, don't indicate that a player's performance was correct when it wasn't.

2. *Give simple and precise feedback to correct errors.*

Don't burden a player with a long or detailed explanation of how to correct an error. Give just enough feedback so that the player can correct one error at a time. Before giving feedback, recognize that some players readily accept it immediately after the error; others will respond better if you slightly delay the correction.

For errors that are complicated to explain and difficult to correct, you should try the following:

- Explain and demonstrate what the player should have done. Do not demonstrate what the player did wrong. Explain what you want, not what you don't want, to have happen.

- Explain the cause or causes of the error, if this isn't obvious; for example, "Your toss was too far in front of you, which caused the ball to go into the net."

- Explain why you are recommending the correction you have selected, if it's not obvious; for example, "Try tossing closer to your front toe so that you contact the ball higher and get it over the net on your serve."

3. *Make sure the player understands your feedback.*

If the player doesn't understand your feedback, she won't be able to correct the error. Ask the player to repeat the feedback and to explain and demonstrate how it will be used (e.g., "Show me how to toss and contact this ball at a high point"). If the player can't do this, you should be patient and present your feedback again. Then have the player repeat the feedback after you're finished.

4. *Provide an environment that motivates the player to improve.*

Your players won't always be able to correct their errors immediately, even if they do understand your feedback. Encourage them to "hang tough" and stick with it when corrections are difficult or when players seem discouraged. For more difficult corrections, you should remind players that it will take time, and that the improvement will happen only if they work at it. Encourage those players with little self-confidence. Saying something like, "You were serving much more consistently over the net today; with practice, you'll be able to get some real movement on the ball and make it difficult for the passers to receive," can motivate a player to continue to refine her skills.

Other players may be very self-motivated and need little help from you in this area; with them you can practically ignore step 4 when correcting an error. Although motivation comes from within, you should try to provide an environment of positive instruction and encouragement to help your players improve.

A final note on correcting errors: Team sports such as volleyball provide unique challenges in this endeavor. How do you provide individual feedback in a group setting using a positive approach? Instead of yelling across the court to correct an error (and embarrass the player) during practice, you can substitute for the player who erred, and then make the correction on the sidelines. This type of feedback has several advantages:

- The player will be more receptive to the one-on-one feedback.
- The other players are still active and still practicing skills, and they are unable to hear your discussion.
- Because the rest of the team is still playing, you'll feel compelled to make your comments simple and concise—which is more helpful to the player.

This doesn't mean you can't use the team setting to give specific, positive feedback. You can do so to emphasize correct group and individual performances. Use this team feedback approach only for positive statements, though. Keep any negative feedback for individual discussions.

Dealing With Misbehavior

Young players will misbehave at times; it's only natural. Following are two ways you can respond to misbehavior: through extinction or discipline.

Extinction

Ignoring a misbehavior—neither rewarding nor disciplining it—is called *extinction*. This can be effective under certain circumstances. In some situations, disciplining young people's misbehavior only encourages them to act up further because of the recognition and attention they get from the coach or their teammates. Ignoring misbehavior teaches youngsters that it is not worth your attention.

Sometimes, though, you cannot wait for a behavior to fizzle out. When players cause danger to themselves or others, or disrupt the activities of others, you need to take immediate action. Tell the offending player that the behavior must stop and that discipline will follow if it doesn't. If the player doesn't stop misbehaving after the warning, you should use discipline, which can sometimes be as simple as not allowing the player to play or practice (if this is important to the player).

Extinction also doesn't work well when a misbehavior is self-rewarding. For example, you may be able to keep from grimacing if a youngster kicks you in the shin, but even so, that youngster still knows you were hurt. Therein lies the reward. In these circumstances, it is also necessary to discipline the player for the undesirable behavior.

Extinction works best in situations where players are seeking recognition through mischievous behaviors, clowning, or grandstanding. Usually, if you are patient, their failure to get your attention will cause the behavior to disappear. However, you must be alert that you don't extinguish desirable behavior. When youngsters do something well, they expect to be positively reinforced. Not rewarding them will likely cause them to discontinue the desired behavior. Remember to try to "catch them being good" as well as catch them "doing it right."

Discipline

Some educators say we should never discipline young people, but should only reinforce their positive behaviors. They argue that discipline does not work, creates hostility, and sometimes develops avoidance behaviors that may be more unwholesome than the original problem behavior. It is true that discipline does not always work and that it can create problems when used ineffectively, but when used appropriately, discipline is effective in eliminating undesirable behaviors without creating other undesirable consequences. You must use discipline, because it is impossible to guide players through positive reinforcement and extinction alone. Discipline is part of the positive approach when these guidelines are followed:

- Discipline players in a corrective way to help them improve now and in the future. Never discipline to retaliate or to make yourself feel better.

- Impose discipline in an impersonal way when players break team rules or otherwise misbehave. Shouting at or scolding players indicates that your attitude is one of revenge.

- Once a good rule has been agreed on, ensure that players who violate it experience the unpleasant consequences of their misbehavior. Don't wave discipline threateningly over their heads. Just do it, but warn a player once before disciplining.

- Be consistent in administering discipline.

- Don't discipline using consequences that may cause you guilt. If you can't think of an appropriate consequence right away, tell the player you will talk with her after you think about it. You might consider involving the player in designing a consequence.

- Once the discipline is completed, don't make players feel that they are "in the doghouse." Always make them feel that they're valued members of the team.

- Make sure that what you think is discipline isn't perceived by the player as a positive reinforcement; for instance, sometimes keeping a player out of doing a certain activity or portion of the training session may be just what the player wanted. Knowing each player and each player's motivation for being on the team may help you decide on the proper consequences or disciplinary actions to take.

- Never discipline players for making errors when they are playing.

- Never use physical activity—running laps or doing push-ups—as discipline. To do so only causes players to resent physical activity, something we want them to learn to enjoy throughout their lives.

- Use discipline sparingly. Constant discipline and criticism cause players to turn their interests elsewhere and to resent you as well.

Coaching Tip

You should involve your players in the process of setting team rules and the consequences for breaking them. Even players under 12 years old are capable of brainstorming ideas about discipline for common situations such as being late to practice, criticizing another player, or talking back to the coach. Coaches should guide the discussion, but the players should be allowed to help construct the team rules and consequences. This will create player buy-in and peer pressure to adhere to the rules. Once you've agreed on a list of rules and consequences, each player should sign an agreement to cement her willingness to abide by them.

7

Coaching Individual Volleyball Skills

This chapter focuses on the individual skills that players need to learn in order to perform effectively in youth volleyball games. Remember to use the IDEA approach to teaching skills: introduce, demonstrate, and explain the skill, and attend to players as they practice the skill (see page 68 in chapter 6). This chapter also ties directly into the season and practice plans in chapter 10, describing the individual skills that you'll teach during the practices outlined there. If you aren't familiar with volleyball skills, you may find it helpful to watch a local college or high school game—or watch recordings of volleyball games—so you can see the skills performed correctly. Also, the Coaching Youth Volleyball online course offered by the American Sport Education Program (ASEP) can help you further understand these skills (you can take this course by going to www.ASEP.com).

The information in this book is limited to volleyball basics. As your players advance in their skills, you will need to advance your knowledge as a coach. You can do this by learning from your experiences, watching and talking with more experienced coaches, taking coaching education courses, and studying resources on advanced skills.

The basic volleyball skills you will teach your players at the youth level include passing (forearm and overhead), serving (and serve receiving), hitting, and blocking. Mastering these individual skills will allow your players to better execute specific plays during the game. These basic skills serve as the foundation for playing volleyball well at all levels.

Passing

In volleyball, the act of gaining control of the ball and moving the ball from player to player is performed using either a forearm pass or an overhead pass. As you learned in chapter 3, an offensive attack is composed of three contacts of the ball. An accurate, skillful pass will allow the setter to place the ball appropriately for the third contact by the hitter to complete the attack.

Coaching Tip

Young players may complain of a "sting" as the ball hits their arms. However, as their technique improves, they won't be swinging their arms at the ball, and the sting will be eliminated as they learn how to absorb the impact. When using a forearm pass, young players should be taught to soften the hit by relaxing the passing platform and bending the knees on contact.

Forearm Passing

The forearm pass is used for receiving serves, hard-driven spikes, down balls, and balls that go into the net. Additionally, at the youth level (and in emergency situations at all levels), forearm passing may be used to set to the hitter, especially when the pass to the setter is too low to set using an overhead pass. The forearm pass is the most common type of pass used in volleyball, and all players must learn how to forearm pass since they will rotate through all positions on the court.

When preparing to make a forearm pass, the player first moves to intercept the ball's path. Keeping the head up to follow the ball as it approaches, the player assumes a ready position with the feet shoulder-width apart and slightly staggered and with the toes forward and knees bent (see figure 7.1). The hands should then be placed together, with the thumbs and wrists together. The fingers and palms can be held in a cupped position (as if going to sip water from the hands), in a fist-wrapped-in-a-fist position, or with the palms facing each other and the fingers interlocked (see figure 7.2, *a-c*). The cupped hand position is recommended because it is generally the most versatile and enables the player to create an even platform with the flat surface of the forearms. This helps ensure that the ball rebounds to the target.

As the player makes contact with the ball, she remains slightly bent at the waist and flexed at the knees; she shifts her weight slightly forward onto the balls of the feet or steps slightly toward the target onto the lead foot to begin

Figure 7.1   Ready position for the forearm pass.

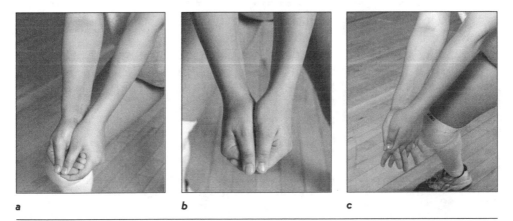

a   b   c

Figure 7.2   Hand positions for the forearm pass: *(a)* cupped, *(b)* fist in fist, and *(c)* interlocked.

the weight transfer (see figure 7.3*a*). The player's head and shoulders should be positioned slightly in front of the knees. The arms should be relaxed and extended in front of the body, maintaining an even platform with the forearms. As the ball drops to approximately waist level, the player contacts the ball on the forearm platform, from above the wrist to below the elbow (see figure 7.3*b*). The ball should be contacted from below and behind the ball. The player stops her arms on contact, maintaining a "frozen" position with the platform, body, and feet all facing the target and with the weight shifted toward the target (see figure 7.3*c*). The platform should remain frozen at eye level or below.

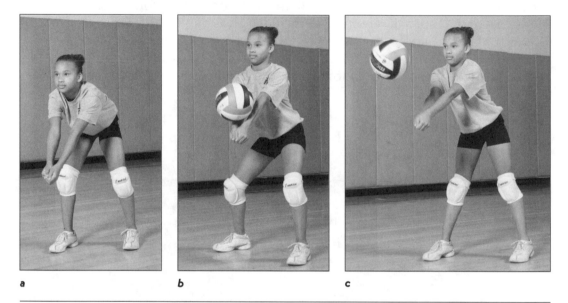

a   b   c

Figure 7.3   Contacting the ball for the forearm pass.

When using a forearm pass, players can also use a technique, called the *platform tilt*, to help direct passes to the intended target. In this technique, the player tilts the forearm platform to deflect the ball toward the target (see figure 7.4). This technique is used when the player is unable to face the target squarely with the hips, feet, and platform. The forearm platform remains flat, but the angle at which the ball is hit and rebounded off the platform is adjusted by dropping the shoulder nearest the target to make the pass possible. The player's weight still shifts toward the target, and after contact, the arms follow through, directing the ball to the target and then freezing.

Figure 7.4   The platform tilt.

Pursuing and Saving

Pursuing and saving an errant pass is one of the more dramatic plays in volleyball. Because a ball is not considered out of bounds or out of play until it lands or strikes an object out of bounds, players can run off the court to track down a ball. They can then pass the ball back into their court so that it can be returned, thus keeping it in play.

All players should be positioned in a ready position, prepared to go after a ball hit in their direction. If a player must pursue a ball, the player should run to the ball with the hands apart (see figure 7.5), because running with the hands together in a passing position will slow the pursuit. As the player nears the errant ball, she should then get her arms into proper passing position, keeping the forearm platform parallel to the ground. She should try to hit a high, playable ball back toward the center of her team's court (or if it is the team's third contact, she should try to send it back over the net between the net antennae). One type of pass that is typically used in this situation is called a *reverse forearm pass*, in which the ball is hit directly over the pursuing player's head back toward the center of his court (see figure 7.6). When hitting the reverse forearm pass, the player should keep his back to the court, rather than trying to twist or turn back to the court as he reaches the ball. Additionally, as the pursuing player is running to the ball, his or her teammates should shift into positions that will allow them to follow and support the expected pass, preparing for the best possible hit on the next contact.

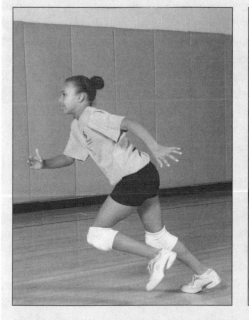

Figure 7.5 Running down an errant pass.

Figure 7.6 Reverse forearm pass.

Forearm Passing Drill

On one side of the net, players take regular playing positions on the court (for 3v3, 4v4, or 6v6, depending on the age group). All other players line up on the other side of the net behind the attack line or end line to take turns in the serving position. When you first introduce this drill, players in the serving position may start near the attack line and gradually move back toward the end line as they build strength and accuracy. The player in the serving position self-tosses the ball and either attacks (standing or jumping) or serves the ball over the net to the passers. The players positioned in the opposite court receive the ball using a forearm pass, directing the ball high and off the net near the attack line to the player in the setter's position. Passing to the setter's position off, or away from, the net rather than right to the net is important so that the setter has a chance to play the next ball without contacting the net (or worrying about contacting the net). The setter uses a forearm pass to direct the ball back to the same passer, who then forearm passes the ball over the net. The player who originally served the ball will chase the ball down as the players rotate and the next ball is put into play by the next server in line.

Overhead Passing

The best-known and most common use for an overhead pass is the set, where the player in the setter's position (see "Player Positions" in chapter 3 on page 27) sets up an attack. The setter determines which player is in the best position for the attack and then uses an overhead pass to place the ball where the attacker can aggressively hit the ball back over the net. The setter should be the best overhead passer on the team; however, all players—regardless of position—will use the overhead pass to play a ball that is higher than face level or to keep the ball in play over the net when an attack is not possible.

To successfully execute an overhead pass, a player must first move into a position to play the ball and must assume the correct ready position. When preparing to set the ball, the setter takes a position in the middle-front or right-front position on the court, one to three meters from the net, and faces the left side of the court. When using an overhead pass for a regular pass and not a set, the player should generally face the opposite-side attacker to deliver the ball in a high crosscourt manner. For both sets and regular overhead passes, however, the player's feet should be shoulder-width apart with the right foot slightly ahead of the left (see figure 7.7). The knees should be slightly bent, with the weight forward on the balls of the feet.

After assuming the ready position and preparing to play the ball, the player will cup the hands above the forehead with a ball-shaped "window" formed by the thumbs and forefingers (see figure 7.8a). The wrists are cocked back, and the fingers are spread and relaxed four to eight inches from the forehead as if holding a volleyball. The player contacts the ball above the forehead with the pads of all the fingers, not with the palm (see figure 7.8b). The player should strive to contact the ball on the lower back side, rather than directly underneath. Whenever possible, the player squares her shoulders to the target before receiving the ball to help ensure that the ball will travel toward the intended target. As contact is made, the player extends the arms and legs upward, while transferring the weight forward toward the target (see figure 7.8c).

A regular overhead pass may be used anywhere on the court by any player. However, the setter is the primary player who will use the overhead pass to set the ball for an attacker, although another player may step in to help if the setter is unable to set the ball. The setter should set the ball two to three feet off, or away from, the net. This will ensure that the attacker has room for a jump and swing and will enable the attacker to hit the ball without contacting the net (see "Hitting" on page 102 for more information). Ideally, a setter should try to place the set in or near the area in front of where the attacker's hitting shoulder will be when

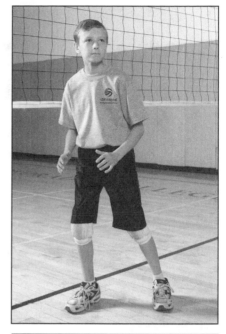

Figure 7.7 Ready position for an overhead pass.

a b c

Figure 7.8 Contacting the ball for an overhead pass.

she swings; the set should be high enough to be contacted at the top of the attacker's reach. Additionally, you should teach setters that they can control the speed at which the attack is made. For example, for older or stronger attackers, the setter can lower the height of the ball on the set, thus cutting down the time between the set and the attack over the net. For younger or less skilled attackers, the setter can slow down the attack by setting the ball higher so that the attacker has more time. Many beginning setters try to place the ball too close to the net, which does not allow the attacker the necessary angles to direct the attack around opposing players who are blocking at the net. You should teach your players that it is better to err on the side of setting too far away from the net rather than too close to it; this will give attackers a better chance of hitting the ball over the net without netting or getting blocked.

Overhead Passing Drill

On one side of the net, players are positioned in the right-back and left-back playing positions. All other players line up behind the end line on the other side of the net to take turns in the serving position. The first player in the serving line tosses, serves, or attacks (self-tosses and hits) the ball over the net. One of the players positioned in the court receives the ball using an overhead pass and passes it near the attack line. Since there is not a setter on the court, the player who did not make the first contact must make the second contact; this player uses a high overhead pass to deliver the ball to the opposite front-row position (right back to left front or left back to right front) to set up the third contact. The player who made the first pass then becomes the attacker and must move to that position to send the ball over the net using an overhead pass (or an attack in older age groups).

Basic Sets

The following are the most common types of sets used to deliver the ball to hitters at the youth level:

- Front outside set—Sometimes called a *four*. The ball peaks at about 10 feet above the net and falls within 1 to 5 feet of the left sideline and a minimum of 3 feet off the net. This is typically hit by the left-front attacker.
- Back outside set—Sometimes called a *five*. The ball peaks at about 8 to 10 feet above the net and falls within 1 to 5 feet of the right sideline and a minimum of 3 feet off the net. This is typically hit by the right-front attacker.

- Middle set—Sometimes called the *high middle* or a *three*. The ball peaks at about 6 to 8 feet above the net and is set into the middle third of the court, a minimum of 3 feet off the net. This is typically hit by the middle attacker but may also be hit by a left- or right-side attacker.
- Deep-court set—Sometimes called a *back-row attack*. The ball peaks at about 8 to 10 feet above the net and is set across the backcourt in one of the three zones (left, right, or middle), anywhere behind the attack line (older or more-skilled players may attack deep-court sets 10-11 feet off the net). This may be hit by any player in those zones, using either a standing spike or jumping attack.

Digging

A "dig" is a type of pass used to save a hard-hit or tipped ball in order to keep the ball up and playable. Typically, a dig is performed using a forearm pass or a variation of this pass—one-handed passes, rolls—in pursuit or emergency situations. The mechanics for a dig are similar to those of the forearm pass; the main difference is that in the forearm pass, a player has time to move, set her position, and play the ball. In the dig, however, the player must react and play the ball with little time to strategically position herself.

When using a dig, after moving into position as best she can, the player should drop as low as possible in order to increase the time she has to play the ball before contact is made. The player bends her knees, keeping her back straight, while moving toward and under the ball and staying in a low position, sometimes even touching the floor (see figure 7.9a). On contact, the player cushions the ball and absorbs the force by relaxing the platform toward the floor and dropping the body's center of gravity. The player directs the ball high and toward the center of the court or toward a different passing target (see figure 7.9b).

a   b

Figure 7.9 Contacting the ball for a dig.

Digging Drill

Players form two teams on the court. Team A consists of three players, and team B consists of one blocker, one setter, and one or two diggers. A coach (or player) serves or tosses the ball to team A from behind team B's end line. Team A makes three hits and attacks the ball over the net into team B's court. The blocker on team B starts at the net but drops off to become a digger when the setter on team A sets the ball to the hitter. If the blocker digs the ball, she will then transition to become the hitter and complete the third contact for her team, and the players on both teams will rotate. If the player does not dig the ball, the coach serves the ball again, and the drill is repeated with players in their original positions.

Coaching Tip
If allowed by your league, a free-ball toss serve is an easy way for younger players, especially those in the 6- to 9-year age group, to put the ball in play. In this method, the server simply tosses the ball over the net using a one- or two-handed overhand throwing motion.

Serving

Besides just putting the ball in play, the serve can be an effective way for a team to score points quickly. This can be done by strategically placing the serve to force an immediate point (an ace) or placing it where the opponent cannot attack the ball. At the youth level, players should learn four types of serves: the underhand serve, the roundhouse serve, the overhand serve, and the jump serve.

Underhand Serve

In youth volleyball, most players learn how to master the underhand serve before learning other types of serves. The underhand serve is easier to control than the overhand serve. Because it doesn't involve a toss, the underhand serve allows beginning players to put the ball in play more easily. However, coaches often introduce the overhand serve once a player is strong enough to throw a ball over the net from the service line with one hand. Once your players are strong enough to use the overhand serve successfully, they should use it whenever possible because it provides a better chance to score points than an underhand serve does.

When preparing to serve, the player may stand anywhere along and behind the end line of the court. The player starts with the feet in a staggered position and the weight on the back (hitting-side) foot. The player is bent slightly forward at the waist. The ball is held at waist level or lower in

Coaching Tip
Many young players use the underhand serve in competition while they are learning and working on other types of serves in practices. This way they can use the underhand serve to be successful in competition until they've mastered the mechanics of more difficult serves.

the nonhitting hand, also called the *shelf*. The ball should be in line with the hitting shoulder and in front of the body (see figure 7.10). The player's eyes are focused on the ball.

To make contact with the ball, the hitting arm is first extended up and backward, and then swings forward as the player drops the shelf hand. The hitting hand makes contact just below the center back of the ball. Contact may be made using the heel of an open hand (see figure 7.11a), the heel and fingers of a half-closed fist (see figure 7.11b), or a closed fist (see figure 7.11c). As the arm swings forward to contact the ball, the player transfers her weight from the back to the front foot. After contact is made, the player's weight remains on the front foot while the hitting arm continues up and toward the target, as if reaching up and over the net. The hitting arm and back leg should remain in line with the target throughout the follow-through (see figure 7.12). After the serve, the player should immediately move forward into the court and assume her defensive position.

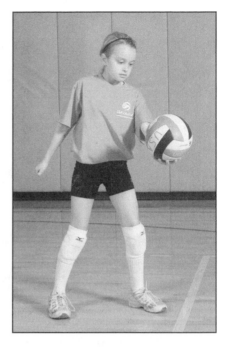

Figure 7.10 Ready position for an underhand serve.

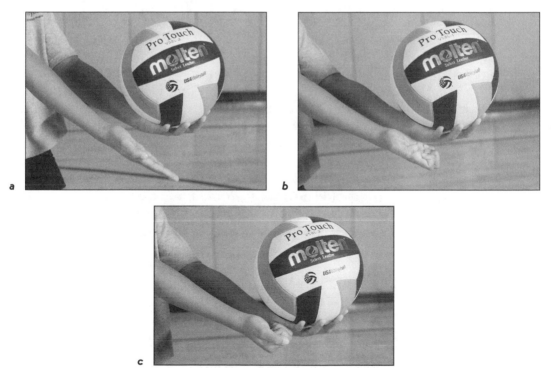

Figure 7.11 Contacting the ball with *(a)* an open hand, *(b)* a half-closed fist, or *(c)* a closed fist.

Figure 7.12   Follow through for an underhand serve.

Roundhouse Serve

A player can generate more power with the roundhouse serve than she can with an underhand serve because the roundhouse calls on larger muscle groups. The roundhouse also uses shoulder and torso torque to add power to the serve. This type of serve involves a toss, so it requires more skill and consistency than the underhand serve. The roundhouse serve is a good lead into the overhand serve because it teaches young players to use shoulder torque (twisting of the body), which will help them understand the motion involved in an overhand serve.

When preparing to serve, the player may stand anywhere along and behind the end line of the court. The player faces the sideline with the front (nonhitting) foot pointing slightly toward the net post (see figure 7.13a). The feet are positioned about shoulder-width apart, with the weight on the back foot. The back foot is pointing toward the sideline. With the nonhitting hand, the player lifts the ball (with little or no spin) slightly ahead of the body and toward the net, in front of where the nonhitting shoulder will rotate toward the ball (see figure 7.13b). As the player lifts the ball on the toss, he swings the hitting arm down and back behind the hip, rotates the shoulders toward the ball, and brings the hitting arm over the head to contact the ball. Contact with the ball is made at the arm's full extension in front of the body (see figure 7.13c). As the arm swings forward, the player shifts the weight forward onto the front foot; he rotates the hips toward the net, followed by the shoulders, so that the body moves into the contact and faces the net after contact (as shown in figure 7.13d). Contact may be made using the heel of an open hand

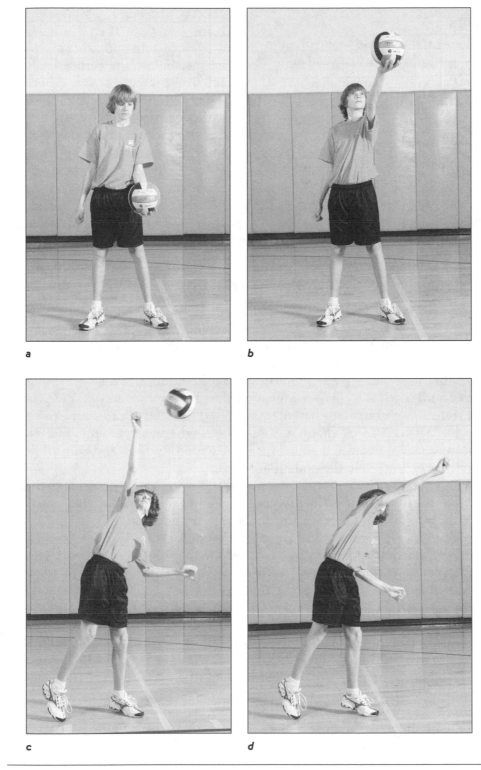

a

b

c

d

Figure 7.13 Roundhouse serve.

Coaching Tip
Because the roundhouse serve involves a toss, beginning players may experience some common problems when they first learn the technique. For example, if the ball goes into the net, they may be tossing the ball too far ahead of their hitting shoulder, or the toss could be too low. If the ball does not go toward the intended target or travels out of bounds on the sideline, the toss may be too far out to the side and not in front of the hitting shoulder. If the ball goes too high or doesn't make it to the net, the toss may be too far behind the body and hitting shoulder.

or the heel of a half-closed fist (see figure 7.11, *a* and *b* on page 91 in "Underhand Serve"). The hitting hand should make contact just below the center back of the ball. The player may use a punching action with no wrist snap and little follow-through to produce a ball that floats in the air (called a *floater* serve), or he may use a wrist-snapping motion and follow-through to produce a ball with spin (called a *topspin* serve). After the serve, the player should immediately move forward into the court and assume her defensive position.

Overhand Serve

Executing the overhand serve can be challenging for young players. To use this serve, a player must be able to toss consistently and must have the strength and coordination to hit the ball over the net using an overhand throwing motion. Since the overhand serve requires more coordination, timing, and strength, you should teach it to players only after they have mastered the underhand and roundhouse serves, or have demonstrated the strength to throw the ball over the net with an overhand motion. The overhand serve, when mastered, is more versatile because it allows for greater speed, power, and control (and better placement) than the underhand serve.

When preparing to serve, the player may stand anywhere along and behind the end line of the court. The player's feet are in a slightly staggered position with the nonhitting foot forward; the knees are bent, and the weight is on the rear foot (see figure 7.14*a*). The player's shoulders are square to the net or slightly open to the sideline. The ball is held in the shelf (or nonhitting) hand at about waist to shoulder level in front of the hitting shoulder. The player's eyes are focused first on the target, then on the ball.

For the overhand serve, the toss is the key to success. A ball tossed too high, too low, too far in front, too far in back, or too far to either side will force the server to "chase" the toss and move out of proper precontact alignment. To make the toss, the player "lifts" the ball approximately 12 to 18 inches out of the shelf hand when the arm is fully extended. The toss should be in line with the hitting shoulder and slightly toward the net (see figure 7.14*b*). As the ball is tossed, the player brings the hitting arm back and up so the elbow is high and the hand is close to the ear; the shoulders rotate back toward the hitting-arm side (elbow toward the back wall). As the ball reaches its highest point, the player—keeping her eyes on the ball—swings the hitting arm forward as fast as possible, leading with the hip and shoulder twist (torque), followed by the high elbow, and then the wrist and hand (see figure 7.14*c*).

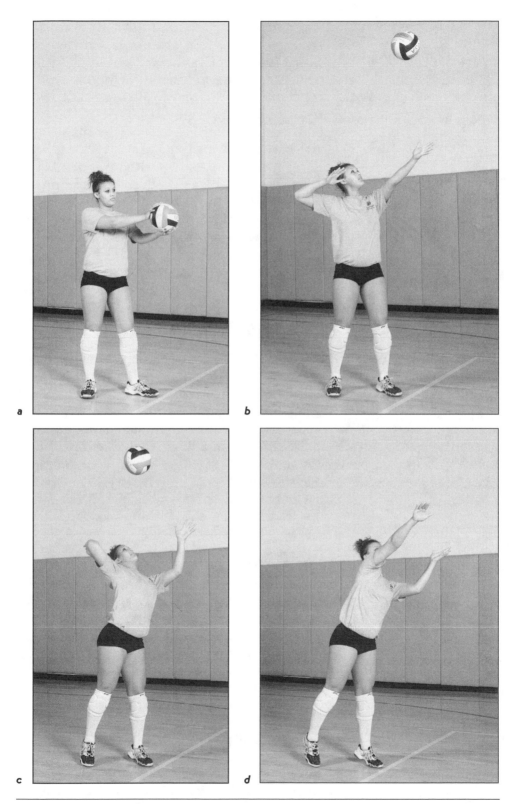

a

b

c

d

Figure 7.14 Overhand serve.

Coaching Tip

Many young players will be uneasy about their ability to serve using the overhand serve. A general test to see if they are capable of using this serve is to check if they can throw the ball over the net from the serving area using a one-handed overhand motion (with shoulder and body torque). If they can throw over the net, most likely they are ready to learn to serve overhand.

Coaching Tip

Older or stronger players may want to adjust their overhand serve to impart topspin on the ball. Although topspin causes the ball to travel in a straight line and can make the ball easier for opposing passers to track, the topspin can also fool an opponent. Topspin causes the ball to suddenly dive toward the floor, which often catches the opponent off guard. To create topspin on an overhand serve, the player tosses the ball slightly higher and straight up (in line with the hitting shoulder), and uses a wrist snap on contact to cause the ball to spin forward over the net.

Contact is made behind the ball (just below center) using the heel of an open hand or half-closed fist. The player uses a "punching" action with little or no follow-through. This type of contact allows the ball to float across the net (floater), causing some indecision and possibly poor passing by the receivers (the player may also use a wrist-snapping motion with follow-through to produce a ball with topspin). As she makes contact, the player transfers weight from the back foot to the front foot (see figure 7.14*d*). After the serve, the player should immediately move forward into the court and assume her defensive position.

At times, players may need to use a short step with the lead foot as the ball is tossed to add some additional power to the serve. This step is often used by smaller, weaker players so that body momentum helps add power to get the ball over the net. Stronger players may also use the step to add even more power to their serves. Additionally, this step can help teach players the initial mechanics for the jump serve. When the step is used, the initial hand and body position is the same as for any serve, and the movement on the serve is "step, toss, swing." For example, a right-handed player stands in her stance with the left foot forward, so she will take a short step with this lead foot, toss the ball, and swing.

Jump Serve

The jump serve is the most advanced of the four types of serves. When performing this serve, the player must jump into the air (similar to an attack at the net) to contact the tossed ball. The jump serve can add more power to the serve and make it even more difficult for opponents to pass accurately. The jump serve is a difficult serve for young players to master, however, because it involves not only proper mechanics (as in the overhand serve), but also accurate timing for the toss, approach, and jump. Coaches should reserve this serve for players who have mastered the overhand serve and the approach used for attacks over the net.

When learning the jump serve, players need to know that two different ball actions can be imparted on the ball at contact—float and topspin—and that there are specific mechanics for each (as in the standing overhand serve). Additionally, players must remember that the toss is crucial in executing a good jump serve. A ball tossed too low, too far in front, or too far to either side will cause the server to move out of proper precontact alignment.

When preparing to serve, the player should be positioned well behind the end line to allow for a toss and an approach toward the net. The player will jump from behind the end line and land in front of the line (into the court) after contact is made. The player's feet are in a slightly staggered position with the nonhitting foot forward and the weight on the back foot (see figure 7.15). The player's shoulders should be square to the net, similar to the ready position for the overhand serve.

For a jump serve that allows the ball to float across the net, a player will most likely use a two or three step approach to help prepare for the jump as the ball is tossed. Performing a jump floater serve is similar

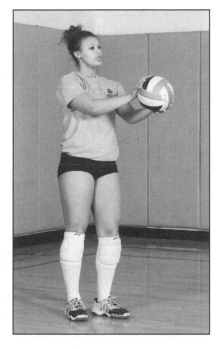

Figure 7.15 Ready position for a jump serve.

to performing a layup in basketball where the ball is lifted up and released on the jump, only the volleyball player will hit the ball with the other hand after the release. For this serve, the toss is lower and the ball is carried longer (held onto until during the final step when it is lifted) and tossed closer to the body than for a topspin jump serve. For a three-step approach, the player steps forward with the front foot (see figure 7.16a), to begin the approach while holding the ball in the shelf hand. After completing this first and then the second step (left, right—if right-handed), and beginning the third (takeoff) step, the player tosses the ball by "lifting" it no higher than 12 to 18 inches above the shelf hand in front of the hitting shoulder while jumping into the air, bringing the hitting arm back with the elbow high and the hand close to the ear. The toss for this serve is slightly in front of the body, as when serving from a stationary position in the overhead serve (see figure 7.16b). Keeping the eyes on the ball, the hitter swings the hitting arm quickly forward, torquing the shoulder, high elbow, wrist, and throwing the hand fast at the ball. Contact is made with the heel of the hand and a stiff wrist (see figure 7.16c) to drive through the back center of the ball to create the "floating" action. After contact, the hitting arm moves slightly through the ball toward the target, freezing with the palm to the target (see figure 7.16d). If using an abbreviated two-step approach for the jump floater serve, the player starts with the first step on the hitting arm side (right foot if right-handed), lifts the ball as she begins the second (takeoff) step, and swings the hitting arm forward as described above.

Figure 7.16 Jump floater serve.

For a jump serve that imparts topspin on the ball, players commonly use a three- or even a four-step approach, similar to a power spike approach, toward the end line as the ball is tossed to help prepare for the jump. For the jump topspin serve, the player tosses the ball by "lifting" it very high and toward the net so the player must chase the toss (keeping the ball well out in front of the body) using the three- or four-step approach (see previous coaching tip on tosses). As the ball is tossed, the player steps forward with the front foot (see figure 7.17*a*). This would be the non-hitting foot for a three-step approach, as shown in figure 7.17*a*, or the hitting foot for a four-step approach. As the ball reaches its highest point, the player completes the final two or three steps of the approach and jumps into the air (see figure 7.17*b*). At the top of the jump, the player—keeping her eyes on the ball—brings the hitting arm back with the elbow high and the hand close to the ear. She then swings the arm forward as fast as possible, throwing the shoulder, elbow, wrist, and hand at the ball. The player contacts the ball with the heel of the open hand, using a snap of the wrist to provide the topspin action (see figure 7.17*c*). After contact, the hitting arm moves through the ball toward the target (palm to target) and follows through "over the net" (see figure 7.17*d*).

After the jump, the server may land inside the court as long as the jump begins from behind the end line and contact with the ball is made before landing. As in other serves, after the player lands, she should immediately move forward and assume her defensive position.

> **Coaching Tip**
> When tossing for a jump serve, players have three options for the toss—a one-handed toss with the hitting hand, a one-handed toss with the nonhitting hand, or a two-handed toss. For younger players, the two-handed toss is easier to control and can be used to teach players how to serve a floater (when using two hands, the ball typically doesn't spin too much so a player doesn't have to counteract the spin). Although most jump topspin servers toss with the hitting hand and most jump floater servers toss with the nonhitting hand, the type of toss a player uses should be her own preference. As a coach, you should allow players to experiment with each type of toss to see which one they're most comfortable with and which one they have the most success with.

Serving Drill

Players pair up with a partner (up to four pairs), and each player takes a position on the opposite side of the net from her partner. One partner is the server, and the other acts as the target. To begin, the server positions at the attack line, and the target player stands anywhere between the opposite attack line and the end line. The server underhand serves to the target player on the other

Figure 7.17 Jump topspin serve.

side of the net (once the underhand serve is mastered, players can progress to roundhouse, overhand, and then jump serves). If the correct technique is used and the ball accurately reaches the target player, the target player calls out "Green light," and the server gets to move one big step back toward the end line for the next serve attempt. If the serve is not performed using the correct technique or does not accurately reach the target player, the target player calls out "Red light," and the server must stay in the same spot for the next serve attempt. Once the server has reached the end line, the players switch, and the target player becomes the server.

Serve-Receive Passing

The reception of an opponent's serve starts the process of your team's attempt to win the point (see "Rally Scoring" on page 35 of chapter 3). A successful serve reception allows your team to begin an attack and win the rally. To successfully receive a serve, players must be able to read and anticipate the direction and trajectory of the ball and determine who will receive it. The sooner it is determined who will receive the serve, the more time that player has to get into the correct position.

The best predictor of the direction of the opponent's serve is the positioning of the server's body. Players who are receiving the serve should look for the angle of the server's shoulders (where they are facing), the direction the forward foot is pointing, the placement of the toss in relation to the hitting shoulder, and the direction that the hitting arm moves. Players should learn that the serve will most likely travel in the direction that the server's shoulders, feet, and toss are indicating. Players should also get into a habit of calling for the ball before it crosses over to their side of the net by yelling, "Mine!" They must quickly move to the correct location and assume the correct body position to receive the serve.

Typically, serves that approach the receiver at chest height or lower should be received using a forearm pass (as discussed on page 82). Less powerful serves, such as those resulting from a slower arm swing or those with a higher trajectory of the ball, should be received using an overhead pass (as discussed on page 86). To judge the trajectory of the serve, players should look for the height of the toss, the height of the elbow on the server's arm swing, and whether the toss is in front of the player's body, directly overhead, or behind the body. If the height of the toss is low, the serve may be a floater, and it may fall in the frontcourt. If the server's elbow is low on the swing, the server will have to hit up on the ball to get it over the net, so the trajectory may be higher and shorter. If the ball is tossed straight up over the body or behind the body, again, the player will have to hit up on the ball to get it over the net, so it may be a shorter and softer serve.

Hitting

A hit—also called a *spike* or an *attack*—is the primary skill used to play the ball over the net. The ball can be hit in several different ways, depending on the speed and height of a set, the location of the opponent's blockers and defenders, and the game situation.

The ready position when preparing for a hit is slightly different from the ready positions for passing or serving. If the hitter, often called the *attacker*, is in a blocking position at the net or has run after the ball for a dig, she must first move to a position several steps from the net. Moving to this location is referred to as *getting available* and helps ensure that the player has room for an approach so she can hit the ball with explosive force. For example, a

Hitting the Crosscourt Angle

The crosscourt angle provides the largest amount of space for a hitter to hit the ball—there is more court space from corner to corner crosscourt than there is from the hitter's position to the corner directly down the line from the hitter (see figure 7.18). To hit the crosscourt angle, a right-handed player hitting from the left front (or a left-handed player hitting from the right front) will begin the approach from outside the sideline of the court. She will angle in (into the court) to attack the ball into the opponent's far corner. If a right-handed player is hitting from the right side of the court, she will start from inside the sideline and take a more straight-in approach to the ball. As she jumps and swings, she will rotate the hips, shoulder, and arm to hit to the opponent's opposite deep corner. The exact opposite would be done for a left-handed player on the left side of the court.

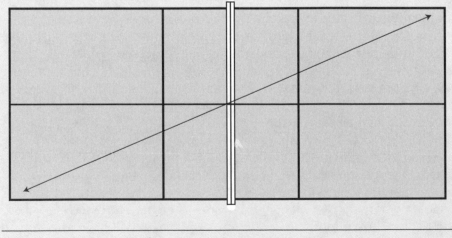

Figure 7.18   Crosscourt angle.

right-handed attacker on the left side should move to a position at or outside the left sideline of the court, about 8 to 12 feet off the net. The player should then assume a relaxed position with the feet slightly staggered, the weight on the back foot, and the body leaning slightly forward at the waist; the arms are comfortably at the sides (see figure 7.19). In this position, the attacker will wait for the set, ready to take an angled approach in toward the net when the set is made. A right-handed attacker on the right side should move to a position at or inside the right sideline of the court, about 8 to 12 feet off the net. The right-side attacker should then assume the ready position and wait for the set. When the set is made, the attacker will take a straight-in approach (or slightly angled approach to the right) toward the net. For left-handed attackers, the positions are reversed—a straight-in approach on the left side and an angled approach on the right side (see "Hitting the Crosscourt Angle" on page 102 for more information).

Attackers typically use a three- or four-step approach for hits, similar to the approach for the jump serve (as discussed on page 96). In a three-step approach for a right-handed attacker, the first step is taken with the left foot (see figure 7.20a); for a left-handed attacker, the first step is taken with the

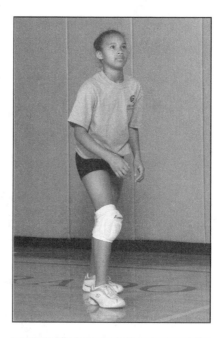

Figure 7.19   Ready position for a hit.

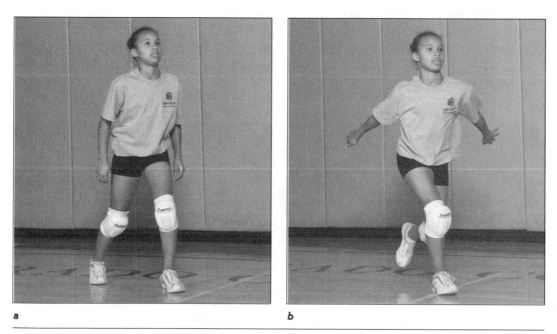

a   b

Figure 7.20   Attacker's three-step approach for a hit (right-handed attacker).

right foot. This first step should be a short, slow step toward where the ball has been set. On the second step (right foot for right-handers; left foot for left-handers), the attacker makes a longer, faster, and more explosive forward movement. On this step, she plants the hitting-side foot on the ground while swinging the extended arms straight back and as high as possible for greater power and leverage on the takeoff (see figure 7.20b). She then takes the last step—a shorter closing step into the jump—with the nonhitting foot. As this closing step begins, the arms drive forward and up in a full sweeping motion to help drive the player high up off the ground to attack the ball. As the foot strikes the ground on this last step, the player should attempt to push off the floor into the jump as quickly as possible to transfer her momentum from the forward approach into the vertical jump.

When contacting the ball, players should imagine the arm as a whip and the hand as the tip of the whip. The snap of the whip begins with the shoulder rotation away from the ball (see figure 7.21), with the elbow of the hitting hand drawn back high and away from the shoulder—elbow to the back wall. In sequence, the shoulder, elbow, hand, and wrist then whip forward again to contact the ball. The attacker makes contact at the top of the center back of the ball with the palm of a firm and open hand; she rolls the palm up and over the ball using the wrist snap action. After contacting the ball, an attacker should follow through quickly by moving the hitting arm through the ball and toward the target and down. If the attacker is hitting in the direction she is facing, the hitting arm should not cross over the body but instead should finish behind the hitting-side thigh. If the attacker's intention is to not hit exactly where she is facing, she can use a deceptive arm swing where the follow-through may be more across the body toward the target. Remind players that a penalty will be called if they touch the net with any part of the body on a hit.

The mechanics previously described are the basic techniques for hitting that you should initially teach to your players. However, once players have learned these basic mechanics, they can then learn how to adjust the contact on the ball for different attacks. The following types of hits are used in various game situations at the youth level.

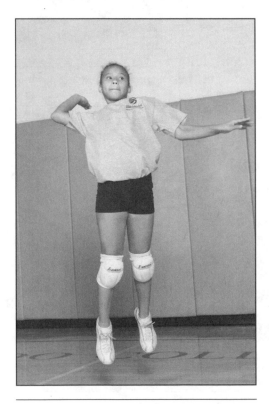

Figure 7.21 Attacker's arm movement before contact with the ball.

Hard-Driven Spike

The hard-driven spike is a forceful hit, usually made on a team's third contact, that is used to put the ball down into the opponent's court. When contacting the ball for a hard-driven spike, the player swings the arm forward quickly, throwing the shoulder, elbow, wrist, and hand at the ball (as described previously). She contacts the back of the ball with the heel of an open hand. At contact, the attacker forcibly snaps the wrist and drives the arm and hand through the ball, following through as described previously. The wrist snap imparts topspin, causing the ball to drop quickly to the floor.

Off-Speed Spike

The off-speed spike—often called a *roll shot*—is a controlled placement of the ball into an open space on the opponent's court, again, typically on the team's third contact. The off-speed spike is often used to deceive the defense by changing up the timing or placing the ball into an area that is not being defended. When contacting the ball for an off-speed spike, the player swings the arm forward quickly, throwing the shoulder, elbow, wrist, and hand at the ball. She contacts the back of the ball with the heel of an open hand, just as she would for the hard-driven spike. However, instead of swinging full speed, just before contact, the player slows the arm swing and slows down the wrist snap. Essentially, the attacker begins with a full swing but then lets up just before contact and hits the ball softly, with slow topspin, directing it over the blockers or to an open area of the court.

Open-Handed Tip

The open-handed tip is another type of hit used to deceive the defenders by changing up the timing of the hit. Hitters use the open-handed tip to try to softly place the ball over the blockers or into other open areas of the opponent's court. When contacting the ball for an open-handed tip, the player swings the arm forward quickly, throwing the shoulder, elbow, wrist, and hand at the ball. She contacts the ball with the finger pads of an open hand, similar to the hand position for an overhead pass. Contact is made just below the center back of the ball when the hitting arm and hand are slightly in front of the hitting shoulder at full arm extension. This hit should direct the ball to barely clear a block and then drop quickly to the floor.

Coaching Tip

The standing spike, also called a *down ball*, is a hit made from a standing position (rather than jumping) anywhere on the court to place the ball into the opponent's court. The standing spike may be used by a back-row player who is in front of the attack line or by any player who may be out of position to make a full approach and jump to hit. The mechanics are the same as the standing overhand serve or an approach and attack (but without a jump). The standing spike can be hit as a powerful hard-driven spike or a slower off-speed spike, depending on the speed of the follow-through.

Back-Row Attack

A back-row attack is generally the same as an attack at the net, but it is hit from deeper in the court. A back-row attack can be hit by any player in her area of the court, from anywhere behind the attack line. It can be performed as a standing spike (see previous coaching tip) or as a jumping attack. When hitting a back-row attack, back-row players must jump from behind the attack line and may land in front of it after contact with the ball. For contact and follow-through, the player may use the techniques for the hard-driven or off-speed spike. Contact is made at a higher point than in a frontcourt attack—with full extension of the hitting arm (as high as the player can reach) and with a wrist snap—so that the ball can travel to and over the net.

Hitting Drill

Players pair up to play 1v1; starting at the attack line, each player takes a position on the opposite side of the court from her partner. The main objective of the drill is for each player (or team when not playing 1v1) to use three contacts to return the ball. For example, when playing 1v1, one player will pass to herself, set to herself, and then attack the ball over the net. Player A starts by tossing or serving the ball over the net to player B. Player B must make three contacts on the ball, sending the ball back over the net to player A. Players should progressively end their three-hit attacks with a standing tip, a standing off-speed hit, and then a standing attack (once players have warmed up enough to jump, they can progress to a jumping tip, a jumping off-speed hit, and then a jumping hard-hit attack). Player A then completes her three contacts, and play continues back and forth until control of the ball is lost or the attack cannot be completed.

Blocking

Blocking is a defensive skill used to stop or slow an opponent's attack at the net. Any front-row player is eligible to attempt to block the opponent's hitter. The objective in blocking is to block an attack so that the ball goes back into the opponent's court or to deflect it high into the air on the blocker's side of the court so that her teammates can play the ball. Performing an effective block requires good timing. The blocker must also be able to anticipate the offensive hitter's intentions and where the ball will cross the net. If blockers misread, misjudge, or mistime the hitter's approach and attack, the block may not offer much resistance. As a result, backcourt defenders will be forced to cover more court area when trying to dig the attack (see "Digging" on page 89).

As a coach, you need to determine whether or not your strategy will include blockers (see pages 117-129 for more information on defensive alignments and playing defense with and without blockers). Note that if you choose not to use the block, an offensive team's attack has a higher probability of earning them a point—without blockers at the net, it may be easier for attackers to drive powerful hits into the defense's court or place hits into open areas of the court where no defensive players are positioned. You must carefully assess the opponent before the game to make an appropriate decision on whether or not to use blockers. The age group you're working with is another important factor. At the younger levels, if players can't reach over the net, blocks quite often may not be necessary. For older players, though, blocks often become an important part of the defensive strategy.

For younger age groups, because of the modified court sizes and smaller number of players on the court, blocking is typically performed by a single blocker and requires only simple footwork. However, for older age groups and 6v6 play, two blockers may be used on one hitter to increase the chance of stopping the attack at the net.

Teaching Blocking at the Youth Level

Some coaches believe that blocking should not be taught if their players cannot get their hands over the top of the net. However, we recommend that you teach young players specific aspects of blocking—such as anticipating and reading the ball and moving to the net. Then, as players grow and become ready to learn how to jump for a block, they will have already learned the basic mechanics leading up to the actual block at the net.

Additionally, as you introduce blocking to your team, emphasize that every member, short or tall, can play an effective role as a blocker. Although taller players have an advantage, shorter players can also block by deflecting and slowing down hard-driven spikes, giving their teammates a better opportunity to play them. Even if your players can't get their hands over the net or can't reach high enough to touch the ball, they can still take away space on the net and force a hitter to avoid hitting in that area of the net. Also, sometimes just having a body in front of the hitter will force the opponents to do something with their attack that they didn't want to do.

When preparing to block, a player should assume the ready position while watching the opponent's pass to the setter. In the ready position for a block, the blocker stands facing the net with the feet approximately shoulder-width apart; the knees are slightly bent, and the weight is on the balls of the feet (see figure 7.22). The hands are held shoulder-width apart at head level between the body and the net. The hands should be open with the fingers spread and the palms facing the net.

Then, when the ball is set to an attacker, the blocker must use a "step-hop-step" foot pattern to quickly get into position across from where the hitter will

Figure 7.22   Ready position for a block.

attack the ball. This is called *fronting the hitter*. It requires blockers to anticipate the location and the angle at which the ball will cross the net so that they can position themselves in front of that angle. Maintaining the ready position throughout the movement, the blocker steps first with the foot closest to the direction in which she intends to move—a step to the right with the right foot or a step to the left with the left foot (see figure 7.23*a*). Next, without crossing the feet, the player pushes off the trailing foot and closes the feet together in the air (see figure 7.23*b*), landing with either a step or a hop so the feet are again shoulder-width apart and the knees bent (see figure 7.23*c*). From this crouched and ready position in front of the attacker, the blocker is now ready to explode up to block the attack. The blocker should remain in this crouched position waiting to jump until after the attacker jumps and begins the arm swing. The farther away from the net

a   b   c

Figure 7.23   Player getting into position for a block.

the attacker is when she contacts the ball, the longer the blocker must wait to jump because of the time it takes for the ball to travel to the net.

As the player jumps to block an attack, she extends the knees to spring up from the ready position, keeping the body parallel to the net and facing the opponent's court. She raises the hands up close to and above the net, if possible; the fingers are spread, with the wrists and fingers held firm. If at the sideline of the court, the outside hand should be slightly angled in toward the middle of the court to deflect the ball back into the opponent's court. If blocking in the middle of the court, both hands should surround the ball (see figure 7.24a). Essentially, the blocker's hands and arms act as a "backboard" for the attacked ball. Players who are smaller, less skilled at the jump, or late jumping to block may perform a *soft block*, where the fingers are still spread, but the wrists are angled slightly backward (see figure 7.24b). This soft block merely deflects the ball up into the blocker's court so that it can be played by a teammate.

After the block, the player lands on both feet, with the knees bent to absorb the force of the jump. The hands are held high to keep them in front of the

a   b

Figure 7.24   Hand position for a block when deflecting the ball *(a)* back into the opponent's court and *(b)* into the blocker's own court.

ball longer and to avoid dragging them into the net on the way down. On landing, the blocker should be ready to move in any direction. If the block deflected the ball back into the opponent's court, the blocker should immediately resume the ready position at the net to prepare for blocking the next attack. If the blocker deflects the ball into her own court and the ball is playable, volleyball rules allow the blocker's team to make three more contacts on the ball. Therefore, if the block is deflected into the blocker's own court, the blocker must be prepared to open up and quickly run off the net to get in position to play the next contact. Then she should assume the ready position for a transition attack if she will have a chance to complete the third contact for her team (the attack).

When teaching players how to block, you should remind them to avoid touching the net and crossing the centerline (as discussed in "Net Play" on page 34 of chapter 3).

Blocking Drill

On one side of the net, players are in playing positions on the court based on the age level of the team (three players, four players, or six players). All other players line up in a single-file line behind the end line on the other side of the net. The first player in line moves into a blocking position near the center of the net. The second player in line serves a ball to the team in the opposite court, who must receive the ball and use a three-hit attack to their left-front hitter. The player in the left-front blocking position must read the opposing hitter's approach, move to front that hitter, and execute the correct skills to make a block. If the player blocks the ball and it deflects back into the opponent's court, she stays in blocker's ready position for another attempt (the second player in line will serve another ball over the net). If the attack goes over, around, or through the player's block—and into her own court—she must execute the proper skills to open up and run off the net to make herself available to attack the ball. This player will then take a place at the end of the line, the second player will move into the blocking position, and the third player will serve. Switch players or positions after each player in line has had a turn.

8

Coaching Transition and Alignments

I n volleyball, an effective transition from offense to defense—and continued flow from defense back to offense—as well as proper team alignment are important for success at any level of play. Without efficient transition and proper alignment, your players will not be in the correct position to receive the ball and run an effective counterattack. This can often lead to points scored by the other team.

Again, remember to use the IDEA approach to teaching skills—introduce, demonstrate and explain the skill, and attend to players as they practice the skill (see page 68 in chapter 6). This approach can be applied to the skills and tactics related to transition and alignments described in this chapter, in addition to the basic individual skills covered in chapter 7. Also, if you aren't familiar with volleyball skills, you may find it helpful to watch a video so you can see the skills performed correctly.

As previously mentioned, the information in this book is limited to volleyball basics. As your players advance in their skills, you will need to advance your knowledge as a coach. You can do this by learning from your experiences, watching and talking with more experienced coaches, and studying resources on advanced skills.

Transition

In volleyball, possibly more than in any other team sport, the transition from defense to offense is swift and fluid. The more efficiently the receiving team gets into its offense (to execute the pass, set, attack sequence), the more likely they will win the point.

When learning transition, your players must first understand that any time your team has the ball on its side of the net (including when a server for the team is preparing to serve), your team is considered to be on offense. Any time the opponents have the ball on their side of the net, your team is on defense (or serve receive when the opponent is preparing to serve; see "Serve-Receive Alignments" on page 129 for more information). Your team must be able to switch—or *transition*—back and forth from defense to offense as the ball moves over the net. For each of your players, this may mean something different. For example, for hitters, transitioning to offense may mean making themselves available for the setter to set the ball to them for the third contact. For diggers, this transition may involve moving from base position to a position where the ball can be dug up to the setter to start the offensive play. And for setters, the transition may require moving from a blocking or digging position into the proper position for setting to the hitters.

Your players must be able to make an efficient transition from defensive positions (i.e., positions for receiving the opponent's contact over the net) into offensive positions. Without an efficient transition, your players won't be set up properly to make a good first contact on the ball to begin their own offensive sequence (pass, set, attack). When this occurs, your team may be forced to return a free ball to the opponent. A free ball is a ball that is not forcefully attacked over the net, but is instead sent over using a forearm or overhead pass. Teams that are continually forced to return free balls to opponents find themselves constantly on defense. These teams will have difficulty scoring points.

As you learned in chapter 7, players should be taught to watch for certain cues to help determine when and where action will occur. For example, when the opponent is preparing to serve, there are specific clues that can help your players better anticipate where the ball will go—such as where the server's feet, hips, and shoulders are facing; where the toss is in relation to her hitting shoulder; and whether the server drops her elbow on the swing. The same applies for players defending an opponent's attack. These players should learn to recognize the attacker's approach and angle (whether she is early or late on her approach), whether the elbow is below the shoulder on the swing, where the shoulder and arm are swinging through, and the hand position on contact. Being aware of an opponent's playing tendencies will help your players better execute individual as well as team skills.

Offensive and Defensive Alignments

The rules of volleyball require all players to be in proper positional alignment (serving order) on the court with no overlapping of adjacent players, either back to front or side to side, before contact is made on the serve. Teams may adjust their basic positioning before the serve based on the opponent they are facing, as long as they don't violate rules about overlapping. Once the ball is contacted on the serve, all players (including the server) may move anywhere on the court in relation to each other. Players will assume specific alignments during play based on team strategy. For example, on offense, players may adjust their alignment based on whether or not the opponent uses a block. Players will also use various alignments on defense, such as blocking or digging positions, free-ball defensive alignment, or positions to defend against a hard-driven spike.

In the following sections, we discuss alignments your team may use when on offense and when on defense. We also include information on serve-receive alignments.

Offensive Alignments

A good offense begins with a good transition pass, so it is important that the setter is correctly positioned to receive the pass and then makes the set to one of the hitters (all of whom should be available in the correct areas of the court) to complete the attack. In this section, we discuss offensive alignments that will help accomplish these things.

As suggested, in youth volleyball leagues—whether played indoors or outdoors on hard, sand, or grass courts—the 6- to 9-year age group usually plays 3v3, the 10- to 11-year age group plays 4v4, and the 12- to 14-year age group plays 6v6.

3v3 Offensive Alignments

In 3v3 play, players maintain a basic triangular alignment on offense (as shown in figure 3.3 on page 28). The server is positioned in the right-back position (RB), the setter is in the center-front position (CF), and the hitter transitions to the left-front position (LF). The three players must rotate into the serving position in the correct order (clockwise) to avoid incurring a wrong server penalty. Before the serve, the three players may stand anywhere on the court as long as the setter (CF) stays in front of the server (RB), and the hitter (LF) stays to the left of the server. In other words, before the ball is contacted on the serve, the RB's feet may not be closer to the net than the CF's feet. Likewise, the LF's feet must not be closer to the right sideline than the RB's feet, and the RB's feet must not be closer to the left sideline than the LF's feet. Once the ball is contacted for the serve, all players may adjust their positions; however, once the rally is completed and a point awarded, the players must return to their original rotational order to await the next serve.

As discussed in chapter 3 (see page 28), in 3v3 play, each of the three players has a primary offensive responsibility and secondary responsibilities depending on which player makes the first contact. In any situation, however, the player who makes the first contact is considered the passer, and this player makes a pass to the setter. The setter should make the second contact. The hitter makes the third and final contact, sending the ball over the net. This player should always put herself in position to attack the set made by the setter.

Coaching Tip

For all age groups, using 3v3 drills or games in practices will give players more opportunities for ball contact and, therefore, skill learning. When playing 3v3, each player will have a one-in-three chance of touching the ball on the first contact, and a one-in-two chance on the second and third contacts (versus a one-in-six and a one-in-five chance, for example, when playing 6v6).

4v4 Offensive Alignments

In 4v4 play, the players' alignment takes on a diamond shape—the setter is at the net, and the three other players are in the backcourt, with the center-back player a little deeper than the other two (as shown in figure 3.4 on page 29). Some teams may choose to position the three back-row players straight across in order to be able to deliver a set to any of the three eligible hitters.

Just as in the 3v3 offense, each player has a primary offensive responsibility and secondary responsibilities depending on which player makes the first contact. Again, the player who makes the first contact is considered the passer, and this player will make a pass to the setter. The setter makes the second contact, usually setting up the hitter for the attack. The hitter should make the third and final contact, sending the ball over the net. This player should always get into position and be available to attack the set made by the setter. In 4v4 play, all three backcourt players are eligible to attack the ball on the third hit. The players who are not making the attack, including the setter, will have support responsibilities in covering the hitter as described in "Hitter Coverage" on the following page.

Hitter Coverage

At all levels of play—whether playing 3v3, 4v4, or 6v6—your players will make minor adjustments to their offensive alignment depending on whether or not the opponent's defensive alignment includes a block. If your hitter will be facing a blocker when approaching for an attack, your team should adjust their positioning to provide coverage against a block that may deflect the attacked ball back into your court. This is called *covering your hitter*. Your passer and setter should move in closer to the hitter, maintaining a low, balanced position so that they are ready to pursue the ball in any direction to make a dig or a forearm pass. If the opponent's defensive alignment does not include a block, your team should be prepared for an immediate return of the ball when your attack is made over the net. Your players should move in a bit closer to the net and immediately shift (transition) into position to play defense in case the ball comes back over.

After passing to the setter, the passer should look to see if the hitter will be up against a blocker. The passer should call out how many blockers are lining up in front of the hitter. After setting the ball to the hitter, the setter should also look to see if the opposing blockers are jumping; she should communicate to her hitter by calling out, "One up," "Two up," or "No one." Although making the adjustment for a blocker at the net is not difficult, it is essential to an effective offense because it enables the team to keep blocked balls in play for another attack attempt. This is similar to getting the offensive rebound in basketball—the more "offensive rebounds" your team controls and keeps in play, the more chances they have to score.

6v6 Offensive Alignments

Naturally, the offensive alignments for 6v6 play are more complex because more players are on the court. Every player must understand her positioning and her individual responsibilities on the court—as well as those of team-mates—for each type of hit or play used by her team's attackers.

As mentioned in "Hitter Coverage," when the opponent uses a block, your players first need to recognize where the block will be set up and how many players (one or two) will be involved in the block. All players share the responsibility of covering the ball when a block occurs. Your team will assume different alignments based on whether your attack—and therefore the opponent's block—is going to be from the right or left side of the court (see figure 8.1). For older players, most blocks are deflected downward between the net and the attack line because blockers are taller and can jump higher. These blockers are able to deflect the ball down into the hitter's court. As a result, your team's alignment should push forward to protect that immediate area around the attacker. If the left-front attacker receives the set, the setter and left-back player will share responsibility for picking up a ball blocked 10 feet

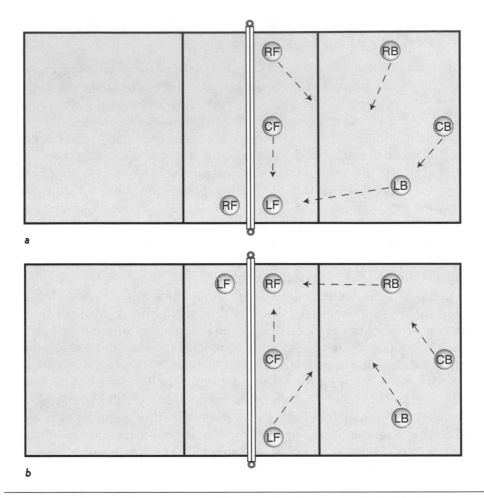

Figure 8.1   Offensive alignment for 6v6 play: *(a)* right-side attack and *(b)* left-side attack.

or closer to the net. If the right-front player receives the set, then the setter and right-back player will have primary responsibility for covering this area.

Although these alignments are desirable, they are not always possible because of the speed of the developing action. Sometimes players may not be able to get to these coverage positions because they have misread, misjudged, or mistimed the play. If this occurs, the players should stop moving toward these positions as soon as their attacker makes contact with the ball, and they should anticipate that the ball may deflect off the opponent's block. Once the attacked ball is blocked, the players must read and react to the deflection to pursue the ball. The players closest to the attacker will most likely have the best opportunity to respond to a blocked ball; however, the players who are farther away must also be ready for and alert to balls deflected higher and deeper into the court.

When the opponent does not use a block, the alignment that your team uses will be similar to the alignment described previously in "Hitter Coverage" on page 115. To be prepared for an immediate return of the ball when your attack is made over the net, players should move in a bit closer to the net behind the hitter and immediately shift (transition) into position to play defense in case the ball comes back over the net (see figure 8.2). In other words, assuming the opponent's defenders will dig your team's attack, your back-row players can work their way back into their defensive positions since there is no threat of the attack getting blocked.

In 6v6 play, the setter will usually be the middle-front player, so all players will know who is responsible for making the second contact and setting the attacker. This allows other players to focus on their individual areas of responsibility—either getting available to attack or getting ready to cover a different hitter who receives the set and may be blocked.

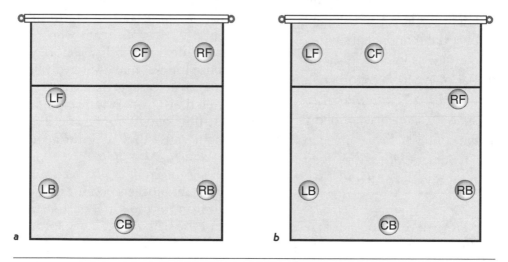

Figure 8.2 Offensive alignment for 6v6 play when the opponent does not use a block: *(a)* right-side attack and *(b)* left-side attack.

Defensive Alignments

Successful team defense is largely a matter of positioning or aligning your players for the opponent's expected attack. Defensively, you must decide your team's strategy based on how your players can best counter the opponent's strengths—and then put your players in the best position to do so. Keep in mind that some opponents will depend on their hitters to make aggressive attacks that score points, while others may prefer to mix up their attacks by hitting hard-driven spikes combined with off-speed hits or tips. As a coach, you must be aware of your opponent's tendencies and watch for times when it might be wise to adjust your team's defensive alignment.

As mentioned previously, your defensive strategies depend on two things: the type of opponent you face and the ability of your team. Always ask, Does this attack deserve a block? And, if so, ask yourself, Do I have players on my team who are capable of blocking? You may want to use blocks when you face opponents who are likely to have a strong attack—for example, teams that include

Coaching Tip
A basic rule in covering the court is that a backcourt defender should never be directly behind or beside a teammate. In other words, no defender should be lined up directly behind the blocker, since the blocker should already be protecting that part of the court behind her. Instead, the backcourt defender (digger) should line up so that if she walked straight forward toward the opponent's hitter, she would end up shoulder to shoulder with her own blocker at the net. This is referred to as being *outside the blocker's shadow*. If the players follow this rule, the court will be balanced in defensive coverage with fewer open spaces for opponents to attack.

bigger players or players who are especially skilled as passers and hitters. When you choose to use blockers, you have essentially determined that the opponents are capable of hitting the ball down into your court with force. Including blocking in your team defense will challenge opponents to either hit over or hit around the block. This may force the hitter to hit a shot that she is less capable of scoring on, or at the very least, may serve as a distraction for the hitter.

However, when deciding whether to use blocks, you must also determine if you have players on your team who have the necessary blocking ability. Before you choose to use blocks, make sure you have players who can at least get their wrists over the net when they jump. Players who can't extend over the net will not be as effective at blocking because they will not be able to stop the attack.

That being said, smaller players can still serve a purpose as blockers because they can position in front of the hitter as a distraction, force a soft block, or at least touch part of the ball, taking away some of its force. However, at the younger levels, playing defense without a block is often the better decision because most players are smaller and not as strong at the basic skills. And opponents who do not have skilled hitters probably do not warrant a blocking defense anyway. Furthermore, if your team is especially skilled at digging, you can accentuate that ability by choosing not to block and therefore having more players involved in digging. For older levels such as the 12- to 14-year age group, you may be more likely to use blocking as part of your team defense because of the players' skill level, size, and jumping ability.

Base Position

The defensive base position is the position your team will hold until it is determined whether the team should move into a blocking formation or move off the net into a dig or free-ball formation. To start, you must understand that your team has three basic options available when they are on defense:

1. *No blockers.* All players are positioned in the areas of the court that are most likely to be attacked so that they are available to dig the attack.

2. *One blocker.* Typically, the blocker should move into position in front of the hitter's most likely or favorite shot (usually crosscourt). The other players are positioned in the areas of the court that are not covered by the block in order to dig the attacked ball if it is not blocked. These players should be located where they can see the attack taking place and where the attack is most likely to fall.

3. *Two blockers.* Typically, these blockers will move into a position in front of the hitter if the attack warrants it. They will try to take away the hitter's strongest or favorite shot, as well as some additional net space. The other players are positioned in the areas of the court that are not covered by the block in order to dig the attacked ball if it is not blocked. These players should be located where they can see the attack taking place and where the attack is most likely to fall.

Usually, your team will know which defensive alignment (one, two, or no blockers) they will be using because you, the coach, will have decided and communicated this before the game begins. At times, you may call block or no block assignments out to the team during play. You may also allow the team captain to decide whether or not the team will use a block based on what she is observing on the court—the strengths of the opponent's attackers, the quality of the set delivered to them, or the quality of the opponent's first pass to the setter. Even when the coach has preassigned a blocking alignment, the block may be called off (by the coach, the captain, or the setter) if the first pass or the set is to the opponent's backcourt area and is not likely to be strongly attacked. Following are the base defensive positions for 3v3, 4v4, and 6v6 play.

3v3

In 3v3 play, players don't usually block, so the base position is a 0-3 alignment (see figure 8.3). No blockers are assigned to try to stop the attack at the net; all three players are positioned as diggers. All three should be facing the attacker's line of approach and should be positioned fairly deep in the court, ready to dig a hard-hit ball. The diggers should maintain a body position that will allow them to quickly push off and run forward in case the hitter hits a softer, shorter attack.

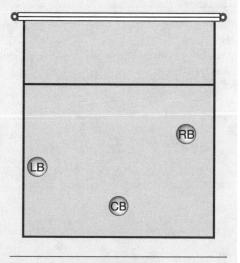

Figure 8.3 0-3 alignment.

4v4

In 4v4 play, the base position is typically the 0-4 alignment (see figure
8.4), where one player stays near
the net to cover short attacks (or to
set the second contact if a teammate digs the ball) and the other
three players are diggers. Once the
set is made by the opponent and
their hitter has been identified by
the defenders, the defending setter
will take a step or two off the net;
she will stop near the attack line
and turn to face the hitter in case of
a short attack. The three diggers are
positioned the same as the diggers
in the 3v3 base alignment—they are

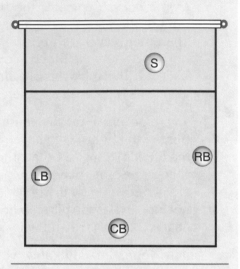

Figure 8.4 0-4 alignment.

facing the attacker's line of approach and positioned fairly deep in the court,
ready to dig a hard-hit ball. The advantage here is that you will have one
player up close to the attacker to dig any tips or off-speed hits and three
diggers behind to dig the hard-driven attacks.

6v6

In 6v6 play, the base position is either a 1-0-5 alignment (see figure 8.5a)
or a 1-1-4 alignment (see figure 8.5b). In the 1-0-5 alignment, one player is
at the net (usually the setter), and the five other players act as diggers and
are positioned for deeper hits. In the 1-1-4 alignment, one player is at the

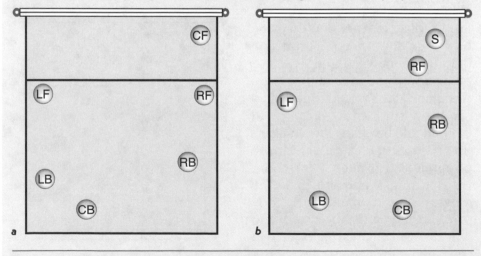

Figure 8.5 *(a)* 1-0-5 alignment and *(b)* 1-1-4 alignment.

net (usually the setter), and one digger is assigned to cover short areas in the middle of the court for tips or deflections; the four other players act as diggers and are positioned deeper in the court for hard-driven attacks. The advantage of the 1-1-4 alignment is that your team will have a better chance to defend against both a short, soft attack and a deep, hard-driven attack. If the hitter changes up to a soft shot to go over or around the blocker, two defenders are there to dig hits to the short court or middle of the court, plus four others are positioned to run down and dig balls hit deeper. The 1-0-5 alignment would be effective when the opponents are powerful attackers and do not use tips or off-speed hits very often.

Defensive Alignments With a Block

If you choose to use blockers as part of your defensive strategy, once the opponents have set the ball to one of their attackers, your blockers will need to move into position to block the attacker's shot. You should teach your players three different blocking alignments that correspond to the three types of offensive attacks they will face: power-spike alignment, off-speed hit or tip alignment, and free-ball alignment.

Power-Spike Alignment   When playing against a team with an aggressive hitting attack, your team should assume a power-spike alignment on defense.

In 3v3 play, your blocking alignment should focus primarily on a power spike coming from crosscourt because this is the most likely shot that will be made. Your blocker should strive to keep this spike from crossing the net.

In this situation, you should use a 1-2 alignment (see figure 8.6). The setter (S) is at the net blocking, the hitter (H) covers the short angle that is open around the block, and the passer (P) covers any ball hit down the line (balls that the hitter hits around the outside hand of the blocker). Balls hit over the block (the setter) will have a higher trajectory, allowing time for the passer and the hitter to communicate and cover this area.

In 4v4 play, your blocking alignment against a power spike will be similar to the base position (as shown in figure 8.4). In the power-spike alignment, which is the 1-3 alignment, one player (usually the setter) is assigned to block

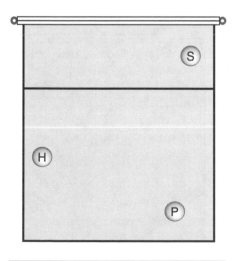

Figure 8.6   Power-spike defensive alignment with a block for 3v3 play.

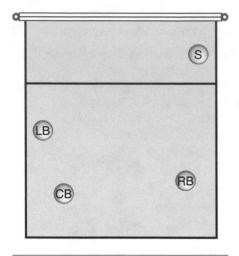

Figure 8.7   Power-spike defensive alignment with a block for 4v4 play.

the attacker at the net, and the other three players are diggers (see figure 8.7). The blocker will front the attacker who receives the set. The three diggers should be facing the attacker's line of approach and should be positioned fairly deep in the court, ready to dig a hard-hit ball. The advantage of this alignment is that you will have one player trying to stop the attack at the net (and possibly score an immediate point) and three additional players covering the ball if it gets past the blocker.

In 6v6 play, either of the two options described for the base position can be used as your power-spike alignment. In the 1-0-5 alignment (as shown in figure 8.5a on page 120), one player (usually the setter) is at the net to block the attacker, and the five other players are positioned deeper in the court to dig balls that get past the blocker. In the 1-1-4 alignment (as shown in figure 8.5b on page 120), one player is at the net (usually the setter), one player is assigned to cover short areas in the middle of the court for tips or deflections, and the four other players are positioned deeper in the court for hard-driven attacks.

With older or more skilled players, you can move on to using alignments with two blockers at the net, such as the 2-1-3 or 2-0-4 alignments. You may use these alignments if you determine that two blockers are needed to stop a more accomplished hitter who consistently hits hard and deep to score. In the 2-1-3 alignment (see figure 8.8a), two blockers are at the net in front of the hitter, one digger is positioned in the short court for tip coverage, and

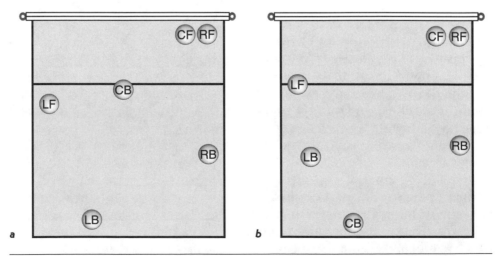

Figure 8.8   *(a)* 2-1-3 alignment and *(b)* 2-0-4 alignment for power-spike defense.

three diggers are in the backcourt. This alignment is strongest against a team that uses tips and off-speed spikes to the middle of the court. When using the 2-1-3 defense, the base position calls for one player—usually the center-back player—to start in the middle of the court near the attack line. The two attackers and the setter stay at the net, anticipating an attack from the opponent's hitter in their zone and ready to move to make the block. The remaining two defensive players position themselves 15 to 20 feet from the net, close to their respective sidelines.

In the 2-0-4 alignment (see figure 8.8b), two blockers are at the net in front of the hitter, and four diggers are positioned in the backcourt. This alignment is most effective against a powerful attacking team that doesn't tip much (which is why no defensive player is positioned in the short court) but hits harder and deeper into the court. The center-back player starts a step or two in front of the end line in the center of the court (she is the deepest of the three back-row players). The remaining two defensive players position themselves 15 to 20 feet from the net, close to their respective sidelines. In this alignment, your players are better able to cover the outer, deeper areas of the court where power spikes will often land.

Off-Speed Hit or Tip Alignment   As described on page 105, an off-speed hit is a slower, softer hit that typically falls into a targeted part of the court where no defenders are located. Opponents who have been blocked often or opponents whose players have slow approaches will often look to use a tip or off-speed hit to avoid the blockers. They will attempt to place the ball in open parts of the court in hopes of scoring points. When opponents read your block and use off-speed hits to avoid the block, your players must anticipate the situation, read the attack developing, and move quickly into the proper position to effectively dig the short or soft attack.

Offensively, the player who will play the ball depends largely on where it is placed on the set and which player has the best angle to make the next play. Therefore, watching the attacker is usually the best way for the defense to know where to position themselves for making the dig. In other words, the defenders must first determine whom the attacker is, then they must read what the attacker will do once she swings and makes contact with the ball. Only then can the defense move into the appropriate off-speed hit alignment to pick up the dig. For example, an opponent's attacker is likely to use an off-speed hit if her approach is slow, her arm swings slowly, or her elbow is low on the arm swing. Communication among your team is also essential in defending this type of hit. Calling out "Tip!" will enable everyone to check who has the best angle and the best chance of digging the ball.

In 3v3 play, the defensive alignment against an off-speed hit or tip requires the setter (S) to be in a position at the net to try to block or deflect any type of offensive attack (as in the 1-2 alignment for a hard-driven spike shown in figure 8.6 on page 121). As previously discussed, when the off-speed attack is recognized, the passer (P) moves in to cover the hit falling over and behind

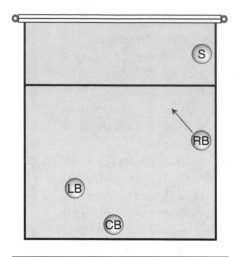

Figure 8.9 Off-speed hit defensive alignment with a block for 4v4 play.

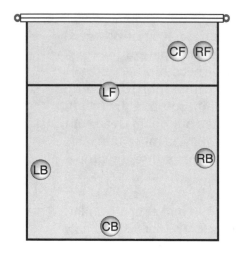

Figure 8.10 Off-speed hit defensive alignment with a block for 6v6 play.

the setter's block. The hitter (H) covers the backcourt area for any deeper off-speed hits or tips.

In 4v4 play, the defensive alignment against an off-speed hit or tip requires the setter (S) to be in a position at the net. When the right-back player reads the off-speed hit, she releases forward to the center of the court toward the attack line (see figure 8.9). In some cases, the right-back player may even start in a position up behind the setter if the team expects the opponents to attempt off-speed hits to the center of the court. The remaining two players split the court to dig the deeper shots, as necessary.

In 6v6 play, the defensive alignment against an off-speed hit or tip is essentially the same as the 2-0-4 alignment (shown in figure 8.8*b* on page 122), with the only difference being the positioning of the left-front player (see figure 8.10). In this alignment, the left-front player should position closer to the middle of the court and near the attack line. This will enable the player to assume more responsibility for digging the off-speed attack since these attacks are primarily directed to the middle of the court. For example, if the attack is from the opponent's left side (your right side), the center-front (CF) player will move toward the right-front (RF) player to form the block. The left-front (LF) player should drop off the net and along the attack line, covering any short balls to the middle of the court. The center-back (CB) player, who will be responsible for balls hit deep or off the block, positions in the middle of the end line. The left-back (LB) and right-back (RB) players should be 18-20 feet from the net and close to their respective sidelines; their movements will be primarily forward toward the attacked ball. If the opponents attack from their right side, simply reverse these positions. If the opponents attack from the middle zone of the net, the center-front and usually the left-front player will block, with the other front-row player dropping back toward the attack line to cover tips or hits off the block. If blocking with only one player, then both the right- and left-front players would drop back, covering short balls to the right- and left-front areas and leaving the center-front player to block the attacker at the net.

Free-Ball Alignment   Free balls do not require a block, so the setter stays at the net and all other front-row players drop back to the attack line.

Defensive Alignments Without a Block

If you decide that your team defense will not include a block, you must consider where to position your players so that they can successfully defend against attackers who do not have to hit around a block. You should teach your players three different alignments for playing without a block: free-ball alignment, power-spike alignment, and off-speed hit or tip alignment. These alignments correspond to the three types of third contacts that your players will need to defend against.

Free-Ball Alignment   A free-ball alignment is used primarily when the opponent has little or no chance of spiking the ball down on your defense—instead, the opponent's third contact on the ball is hit from below the top of the net, typically with a forearm or overhead pass. A free ball may result from a misdirected set that goes over the net instead of to the attacker. The offensive team may also hit a free ball when they are unable to attack the ball and are forced to pass it over the net simply to keep it in play. Free balls are usually hit high, soft, and deep; therefore, a block is not effective in defending a free-ball attack.

In 3v3 play, all three players have areas of responsibility against a free ball. Similar to the 0-3 defensive alignment without a block, the hitter (H) moves back to cover the crosscourt angle if the ball moves in this direction. The passer (P) covers the middle of the court, and the setter (S) backs off the net, awaiting the free ball over the net (see figure 8.11). Because the free ball is usually a higher, softer hit ball, there should be sufficient time for the hitter or passer to get to the ball for either a forearm or overhead pass. The setter should also then have time to get back to the net to set the ball on the second contact. After the ball is received and the first contact is made, the hitter must get prepared for the attack by assuming her hitter's ready position while watching the setter and the ball.

In 4v4 play, the free-ball alignment is generally the same as in 3v3 play, except the setter typically stays closer to the net in her setter position to take the second contact. The other three players are all positioned in the backcourt, and one of the three will play the free ball (see figure 8.12).

In 6v6 play, your players will position in a spread arrangement where the players form a W shape (see figure 8.13). In this alignment, the left-front (LF) and right-front (RF) players back

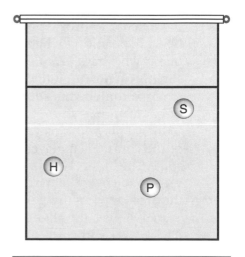

Figure 8.11   Free-ball defensive alignment without a block for 3v3 play.

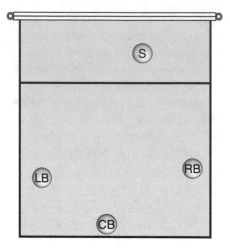

Figure 8.12   Free-ball defensive alignment without a block for 4v4 play.

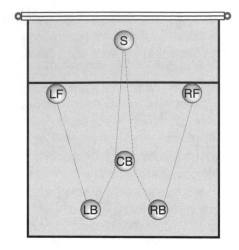

Figure 8.13   Free-ball defensive alignment without a block for 6v6 play.

off the net to the attack line to play any free ball in front of them. The center-back (CB) player moves up into the middle of the court since the center-front player is the setter (S) and will remain at the net to set on the second contact. Any ball that goes deeper into the court should be played by the backcourt players (the right-back or the left-back player), who are each responsible for one-half of the backcourt area.

Power-Spike Alignment   If your team is defending a power spike or hard-hit attack without a blocker, you have the advantage of being able to place more players in the deep crosscourt area of the court. This is the area where the attack will most likely be directed. Having more players in the area enables the defense to provide better coverage and increases the chances of a player being in position to dig the ball up to the setter. In 4v4 and 6v6 play, the only player who stays near the net in this alignment is the setter. The setter drops slightly off the net and turns sideways to the net with her eyes on the attacker, ready to run down a short ball or to pursue and set a ball that is dug by one of her teammates.

In 3v3 play, your players will back off the net in position to cover the angles of the court. Each player should be in a ready position to dig a hard-driven spike. The hitter (H) will cover the crosscourt angle, the setter (S) will drop off the net to cover the hard attack down the line, and the passer (P) will cover the area between these two angles (see figure 8.14).

In 4v4 play, the alignment is essentially the same as for 3v3 play. The left-back player will cover the crosscourt angle, the center-back player will drop deep to the end line, and the right-back player will drop deep to cover the hard attack down the line. However, for 4v4, the setter will either stay close to the net to make the second contact or pull off the net just inside the attack line to help cover a tipped ball (see figure 8.15).

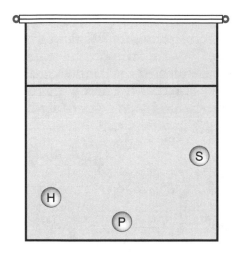

Figure 8.14 Power-spike defensive alignment without a block for 3v3 play.

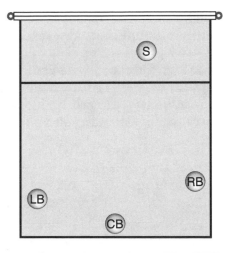

Figure 8.15 Power-spike defensive alignment without a block for 4v4 play.

In 6v6 play, the right-back (RB) player covers the deep sideline shot, the center-back (CB) player covers the deep middle, and the left-back (LB) player covers the deep crosscourt shot, which is where the attack will most likely be directed at most levels of play. The right-front player (RF) and the setter (S), who would normally be blockers, will drop back to the attack line to cover short balls. The left-front (LF) player also drops back from a blocking position at the net to the attack line, near the sideline, to cover the short corner (see figure 8.16).

In the power-spike alignment without a blocker, your defenders should have more flexibility than when blockers are used. Without a block, the back-row players will need to make adjustments to move into positions they think will effectively defend the opponent's attack. Your players must read the opposing hitter's cues to where she will hit, and then move into that secondary position to dig the ball. The sequence for all diggers should be to get into base position, react to the set, and move into their initial defensive alignment. They will then read the hitter's approach, swing, and direction—and then read, react, and move to the ball for the dig. The placement of the front row also becomes important to consider, since these players will not be blocking. In this situation the two front-row players closer to the point of attack (CF and RF) will pull off the net five to six feet to defend against

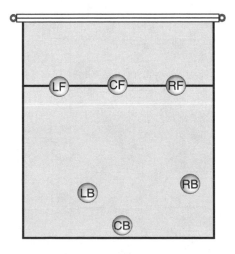

Figure 8.16 Power-spike defensive alignment without a block for 6v6 play.

off-speed attacks. The blocker farthest from the point of attack (LF) in essence becomes another back-row defender, covering crosscourt shots along with the left-back player (LB). Having the center-front and right-front players responsible for shorter balls enables the back-row defenders to concentrate on any hard-driven spikes or any high balls that go deep into their court. Be sure to set parameters for each back-row defender, however, so that no confusion arises among defenders about who should dig a particular ball.

Off-Speed Hit or Tip Alignment   To defend an off-speed hit or tip without a blocker at the net, players move in closer to the net to pick up the short, soft ball that results from these types of hits. As discussed in chapter 7, opponents will sometimes use an off-speed hit to throw your team off balance because your players will typically expect a hard-driven or deep ball on an opponent's attack. Defensively, front-row players need to learn how to anticipate the development of an off-speed attack based on the cues that the opponents give away—for example, the placement and quality of the pass and the set, the attacker's approach speed, and the height and speed of the arm swing on the attack. Encourage the back-row defenders to take responsibility for any off-speed attacks that fall between the front and back rows. A player who is moving forward toward the ball has a better chance of making a well-placed dig to the setter than a player who is moving backward on the court.

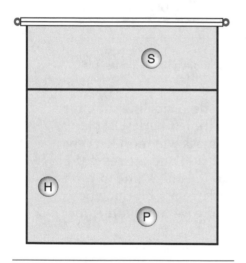

Figure 8.17   Off-speed hit or tip defensive alignment without a block for 3v3 play.

In 3v3 play, the alignment is essentially the same as the 0-3 base position or free-ball alignment. The hitter (H) covers the crosscourt angle in case the ball moves in this direction. The setter (S) covers the area between the attack line and the net (also called the *short court*). The passer (P) plays the deep area of the court between the attack line and the end line (see figure 8.17).

In 4v4 play, the alignment is a 0-4 alignment that is similar to the one used in 3v3 play. The left-back (LB) player covers the crosscourt angle in case the ball moves in this direction. The center-back (CB) player covers the deep center of the court, playing slightly toward the crosscourt side. The right-back (RB) player plays the deep area of the court between the attack line and the end line. The setter (S) covers the area near the net between the attack line and the net (see figure 8.18).

In 6v6 play, the off-speed hit alignment is similar to the power-spike alignment without

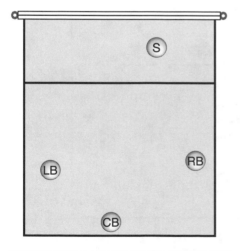

Figure 8.18   Off-speed hit or tip defensive alignment without a block for 4v4 play.

a blocker (as shown in figure 8.16 on page 127). The right-back (RB) player covers the deep sideline, the center-back (CB) player covers the deep middle, and the left-back (LB) player covers the deep crosscourt area. The two front-row players, CF and RF, who would normally be blockers, will drop off the net to cover the area between the attack line and the net in front of the hitter. The left-front (LF) player drops off the net from her blocking position; she comes in about three to four feet from the short corner, ready for hard angle hits or ready to run forward for soft shots.

Serve-Receive Alignments

You must plan out your team's serve-receive alignment so that your players are in the proper position to receive the opponent's serve. Essentially, this involves designating certain players—those who are proficient passers—to take all first contacts on the opponent's serve and placing these players in position to do so. If a team can pass the serve consistently in a playable manner from their serve-receive alignment, they will be better at keeping their opponents from scoring on the serve. Effective passing on the serve receive will also enable the team to generate their own offensive attack and to score points on transition. The most common serve-receive alignments at the youth level are the two-player, three-player, and five-player serve-receive alignments.

Two-Player Serve Receive

The two-player serve receive is the typical alignment used in 3v3 play. Even in 4v4 or 6v6 play, if your opponent has a weak serving game—that is, few serves that are hard hits or difficult to pass—you can use the two-player serve receive. However, you need to have skilled passers on your team who have above-average abilities to move and anticipate action. Although two passers may not always be enough to handle serves, especially for younger players, the two-player serve receive works well for older players. This alignment gives two players the primary responsibility for every serve that crosses the net. Passing with more than two players can lead to breakdowns in communication as more people try to simultaneously communicate their intentions and cover more seams between players. The disadvantage of the two-player serve receive is that it does not provide opportunities for all passers on your team to get better, unless all players get to be one of the two passers at some point. Keep in mind that if you have three or more players with comparable passing skills on your team, you should probably use them as primary passers and opt for a three-player serve-receive alignment (as discussed in the following section).

Coaching Tip

In youth volleyball, serves often drop between the passers because players don't know the "rules" of who should cover where, or because they do not call for the ball early enough or at all. A good rule of thumb to determine who should pass the ball is this: The passer who can move toward the target and pass should be the player who passes. A player who tries to receive a serve while moving away from the target will have difficulty controlling the pass and directing it to the target.

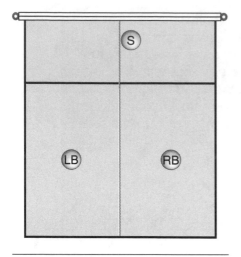

Figure 8.19 Two-player serve-receive alignment for 3v3 play.

In 3v3 play, two players are positioned back in the court to receive the serve. The two players basically split the court in half, and each is responsible for covering serves directed into her half of the court. The third player, the setter, is at the net prepared to set the pass (see figure 8.19). The objective is for one of the passers to receive the serve and pass the ball to the setter without forcing the setter to move very far out of position. This way, the setter can set a good ball for the third contact by the player who did not receive the serve. The passer who doesn't receive the serve should move up toward the net so that she is in position and available to hit the ball that the setter sets.

In 4v4 play, the two best passers on your team should be positioned back in the court to receive the serve. The two players basically split the court in half, and each is responsible for covering serves directed into her half of the court. The other two players are not involved in the serve receive—the setter is positioned at the net, and the fourth player is in a position to attack the set on the third contact (see figure 8.20).

In 6v6 play, the left-back (LB) and right-back (RB) players will typically receive most of the serves. These two players will split the court in half, with each player being responsible for covering serves directed into her half of the court. Although the back-row players have the primary serve-receive responsibility in this alignment, front-row players may or may not be assigned some responsibility for receiving short serves. The player who receives the serve will pass the ball to the setter (CF) so that the setter can set a good ball for the third contact by either the left-front (LF) or right-front (RF) attacker (see figure 8.21).

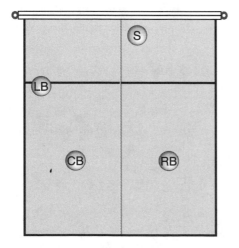

Figure 8.20 Two-player serve-receive alignment for 4v4 play.

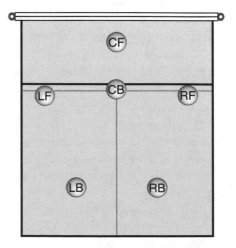

Figure 8.21 Two-player serve-receive alignment for 6v6 play.

Three-Player Serve Receive

The three-player serve receive (in addition to the five-player serve receive that will be discussed later) is a good option if your team has difficulty receiving the serve—that is, the ball goes erratically out of bounds or doesn't reach the setter. This alignment can be used at all levels (3v3, 4v4, or 6v6). The three-player alignment puts more players in position to receive the serve and leaves fewer holes for the server to serve into. Having more serve receivers (such as in the three-player serve-receive alignment) is recommended when working with less skilled or younger players. When teams use a three-player serve-receive alignment, their passers often have comparable passing ability. Sometimes, however, one passer will be slightly better than the others. In such an instance, you may choose to give this passer responsibility for a larger area of the court.

In 3v3 play, a three-player serve receive gives each player equal responsibility in receiving the serve. This helps ensure that all areas of the court (left, middle, and right zones) are covered and that short or deep serves can be defended effectively. In this alignment, the left-side player covers the left third of the court, the right-side player can be assigned to cover either the middle third or the right third of the court, and the center player is assigned to the remaining third. Assuming that the serve is made from the opponent's right-back position, when players recognize that a short serve to the frontcourt area is likely, all three players can move closer to the net—when this occurs, the setter (S) covers the middle zone near the net, the hitter (H) covers the short down the line area, and the passer (P) covers the short crosscourt angle (see figure 8.22a). For example, if the setter makes the first contact receiving a short serve, then the passer (P) would call the ball and set the second contact to the hitter (H) or even back to the setter, who is now an eligible hitter. Again, assuming that the serve is made from the opponent's right-back position, when players recognize that a long serve to the backcourt area is likely, the setter covers the mid to short crosscourt angle, and the hitter and the passer cover the long down the line and the long middle-serving angles (see figure

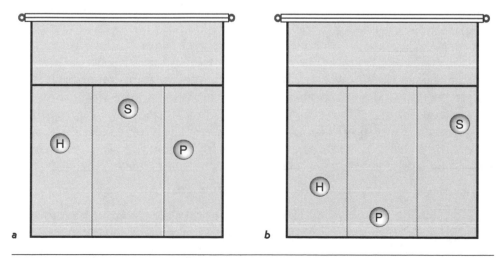

a   b

Figure 8.22   Three-player serve receive for 3v3 play.

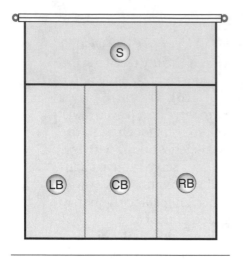

Figure 8.23 Three-player serve-receive alignment for 4v4 play.

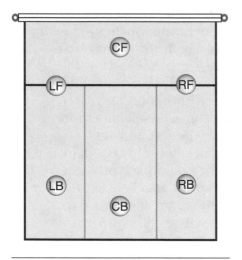

Figure 8.24 Three-player serve-receive alignment for 6v6 play.

8.22*b*). In this instance, the setter is the least likely to receive the serve because the sharp, short crosscourt angle is the most difficult for a server to hit. Therefore, the setter is in the best position to make the second contact (the set) on the pass from one of the other two players. If the setter must move deeper into the court to receive the serve and make the first contact (such as when the server makes the serve from the opponent's left-back area), the passer or the hitter will become the setter. The set should be made by whichever player has the best angle to get the second contact in a hittable position to another player for the spike.

In 4v4 play, a three-player serve receive allows the setter to stay at the net. The other three players split the court into three areas (left, middle, and right), and each player is responsible for covering serves in her area (see figure 8.23). When passers recognize that a short serve is likely, they should step forward to pass the ball with either an overhead pass (if the ball is high) or a forearm pass (if the ball is at waist height). When players recognize that a long serve is likely, they should drop back to get behind the ball in order to pass (using either a forearm or an overhead pass) to the setter for the second contact.

In the three-player serve-receive alignment for 6v6 play, the left-, right-, and middle-back players split the court into three areas (left, middle, and right zones). Each player is responsible for covering serves in her area, from the net to the end line (see figure 8.24). The primary responsibility for passing serves typically falls on the right-back (RB) and left-back (LB) players, but the center-back (CB) player may have equal responsibility or will have responsibility if the serve is long and deep. The front-row attackers (LF and RF) generally do not have serve-receive responsibility unless the serve is very short to their area. The sixth player, the setter (CF), should never pass the first ball in 6v6 play; instead, she should be readying herself to take the second contact on each play.

Five-Player Serve Receive

In 6v6 play, the five-player serve receive is another good option if your team has difficulty receiving the serve. The five-player serve receive can be used when your players' skill level isn't very high or when you want to give more players opportunities to practice the skill of serve reception. Your players need to understand that the more passers that are involved in the serve receive, the more important communication becomes. As a coach, you should take time to practice this with your players. When teams use a five-player serve-receive alignment, their passers often have comparable passing ability. Sometimes, however, one passer will be slightly better than the others. In such an instance, you may choose to give this passer responsibility for a larger area of the court.

In a five-player serve-receive alignment, all players except the setter should be prepared to receive the serve. The left-front (LF), right-front (RF), and center-back (CB) players are responsible for shorter serves, and the left-back (LB) and right-back (RB) players are responsible for deep serves. This is sometimes referred to as a *W serve-reception pattern* (as shown in figure 8.13 on page 126). All players, except the setter, are responsible for some area of the court. The LB and RB players split the backcourt and are responsible for covering serves in their half of the court (to their respective sidelines). Depending on who takes the first contact, the setter will most likely take the second contact, with one of the hitters taking the third contact.

9

Coaching on Competition Day

Competitions provide the opportunity for your players to show what they've learned in practice. Just as your players' focus shifts on competition days from learning and practicing to competing, your focus shifts from teaching skills to coaching players as they perform those skills in games. Of course, the competition is a teaching opportunity as well, but the focus is on performing what has been learned, participating, and having fun.

In previous chapters, you learned how to teach your players the skills of volleyball; in this chapter, you will learn how to coach your players as they execute those skills in competition. We provide important coaching principles that will guide you before, during, and after the game.

Before the Game

Many coaches focus on how they will coach only during the actual game, when instead preparations should begin well before the first play of the game. Ideally, a day or two before a game, you should cover several things—in addition to techniques and tactics—to prepare your players for the game. Depending on the age group you are working with, you will need to create a specific game plan for the opponent based on information that is available to you. This task will include making decisions on specific team tactics that you want to use. You should also discuss pregame particulars such as what to eat before the game, what to wear, when to arrive, and how to warm up.

Deciding Team Tactics

Some coaches burn the midnight oil as they devise a complex plan of attack. Team tactics at this level, however, don't need to be complex—especially for the younger age groups. The focus should be on consistent execution, attacking the ball on offense, and playing good team defense. You should emphasize the importance of teamwork, of every player fulfilling her role in the offensive and defensive systems, and of every player knowing her assignments. As you become more familiar with your team's tendencies and abilities, you can help them focus on specific tactics that will help them play better.

During the week before a game, you should inform players of the tactics that you think will work and that you plan to use in the game. Plan several offensive sets, attacks, and plays as well as the main defense that you want to use in the game. Try to practice these at every practice, and make certain that every player understands these tactics and that

> **Coaching Tip**
> When developing your game plan, keep in mind that your players need to understand what you expect of them both offensively and defensively during the game. Be clear about this in the days leading up to a game. Take time at the beginning or end of each practice to discuss these expectations.

Creating a Game Plan

Just as you need a practice plan for what you will cover at each practice, you also need a game plan for game day. As a coach for youth volleyball, your game plan will vary depending on the age group you are working with. As you begin planning and mapping out how your game days will progress, you should keep the following age-related points in mind.

Ages 6 to 9	• Encourage players to try their best. • Focus on helping players develop their individual skills for team competition. The strengths and weaknesses of the opposition are of little concern at this age. • Although actual games are important, do not spend too much time just playing games without time for proper skill instruction.
Ages 10 to 11	• Focus on helping your team execute the skills they have learned. • Use simple defensive strategies that make it easy for your players to play with each other and execute the techniques and skills learned in practice. • Remind players of one offensive and one defensive aspect they have learned, and ask them to focus on these skills during the game.
Ages 12 to 14	• Players should begin to focus on one or two of the opponent's strengths and weaknesses and should be able to take advantage of this while the game is being played. • Teams will sometimes adjust their play based on the opponent, but the most important thing is still the proper execution of the techniques and skills learned in practice. • Use more complex team offenses and defenses that will take advantage of the opponent's weaknesses.

the team can run them without error. Limiting the number and type of sets and attacks will allow you to repeat them during practice and instill in your players the confidence that they can execute the plays during the game.

Depending on the age level, experience, and knowledge of your players, you may want to let them help you determine the first offensive play or set and the defense that you will call in the game. It is the coach's role to help youngsters grow through the sport experience. Allowing player input helps your players learn the game and involves them at a planning level often reserved solely for the coach. It also gives them a feeling of ownership. Rather than just carrying out orders for the coach, they're executing the plan of attack that they helped decide. Youngsters who have a say in how they approach a task often respond with more enthusiasm and motivation.

Coaching Tip
You should have a preset plan or routine that is used before every game. This can help alleviate nerves and build confidence in your players, especially those in younger age groups. A pregame routine will also help players forget outside concerns and get into the frame of mind to focus on the game.

Discussing Pregame Details

Players need to know what to do before a game, such as what they should eat on game day and when, what clothing they should wear to the game, what equipment they should bring, what time they should arrive, and how the warm-up will be run. You should discuss these particulars with them at the last practice before a game. Here are guidelines for discussing these issues.

Pregame Meal

In general, good sports nutrition begins several days before the competition, but the goal for the pregame meal on game day is to fuel the player for the upcoming event, to maximize carbohydrate stores, and to provide energy to the brain. Some foods digest more quickly than others, such as carbohydrate and protein, so we suggest that players consume these rather than fat, which digests more slowly. Good carbohydrate foods include spaghetti, rice, and bran. Good protein foods include low-fat yogurt and boneless, skinless chicken. Players should eat foods that they are familiar with and that they can digest easily. Big meals should be eaten three to four hours before the game. Of course, players who don't have time for a big meal can use sport beverages and meal-replacement bars.

Clothing and Equipment

As discussed in chapter 3, at the youth level, most teams wear like-colored T-shirts (either long or short sleeved) with numbers (if required) and shorts as the team uniform. Depending on the age group, where the game is played, and how far the team travels to the game, you should typically require that your players bring their uniforms and shoes with them to the game and change into them at the game site. With very young players, you might be better off having them dress at home and travel in their uniforms so that parents can help make sure they haven't forgotten anything.

Knee pads are recommended for youth players. Some players may choose to wear eyewear, athletic braces, or mouth guards for protection and should be allowed to do so as the rules permit. Jewelry should not be worn in the game and is illegal under most rules.

Arrival Time

Your players need to adequately warm up before a game, so you should instruct them to arrive 20 to 60 minutes before game time—depending on the age group—to go through the team warm-up (see the next section for more information on the warm-up). Younger players may arrive closer to game time; this will help keep them focused and prevent them from getting too tired from the excitement of warming up and preparing to play. Following are the suggested arrival times for each age group:

- Ages 6 to 9—20 to 30 minutes before game time
- Ages 10 to 11—30 to 45 minutes before game time
- Ages 12 to 14—40 to 60 minutes before game time

Designate where you want the team to gather as they arrive so you can quickly see who is there, have a quick team meeting, and start the warm-up on time. If you have problems with players coming late to games, you can consider making a team rule stating that players must show up a designated amount of time before the game and go through the complete team warm-up, or they won't start.

Warm-Up

Players need to both physically and mentally prepare for a game once they arrive, and physical preparation involves warming up. We've suggested that players arrive 20 to 60 minutes before the game to warm up (depending on the age group). You will want to conduct the pregame warm-up similar to practice warm-ups. Before game day, you should walk the players through the steps for how they will enter the court and where they will line up for the warm-up.

The warm-up should consist of a few brief games or drills that focus on skill practice in small groups, exercises that involve a range of motion, and basic ballhandling sequences. It should also include overhand throwing or serving drills from close to the net to get the players moving and contacting the ball in a low-impact manner. If no net space is available, any line on the floor can be used to simulate the net.

You should refrain from delivering a long-winded pep talk, but you can help players mentally prepare for the game by reminding them of the skills they've been working on in recent practices and by focusing their attention on their strengths and what they've been doing well. Also take time to remind players that they should work as a team, play hard and smart, and have fun!

> **Coaching Tip**
> Although the site coordinator and officials have the formal responsibilities for facilities and equipment, you should know what to look for to ensure that the game will be safe for all players (see "Facilities and Equipment Checklist" in appendix A on page 166). You should arrive at the game site 45 to 60 minutes before the game so you can check the facility, check in with the site coordinator and officials, and greet your players as they arrive to warm up.

Unplanned Events

Part of being prepared to coach is to expect the unexpected. What do you do if players are late? What if *you* have an emergency and can't make the game

Communicating With Parents

The groundwork for your communication with parents will have been laid in the parent-orientation meeting, where the parents learned the best ways to support their kids'—and the whole team's—efforts on the court. You should encourage parents to judge success based not just on the outcome of the game, but also on how the kids are improving their performances.

If parents yell at the kids for mistakes made during the game, make disparaging remarks about the officials or opponents, or shout instructions to their child or to the team, you should ask them to refrain and to instead support the team through their positive comments and actions. These standards of conduct should all be covered in the preseason parent-orientation meeting, and parents should be expected to follow these standards at all competitions.

When time permits, as parents gather before a game (and before the team has approached the court), you can let them know in a general sense what the team has been focusing on during the past week and what your goals are for the game. However, your players must come first during this time, so focus on your players during the pregame warm-up.

After a game, quickly come together as a coaching staff (if you have one) and decide what to say to the team. Then, if the opportunity arises, you can informally assess with parents how the team did based not on the outcome, but on meeting performance goals and playing to the best of their abilities. Help parents see the game as a process, not solely as a test that is pass or fail, or win or lose. Encourage parents to reinforce these concepts at home.

For more information on communicating with parents, see page 18 in chapter 2.

or will be late? What if the game is postponed? Having a plan and being prepared to handle out-of-the-ordinary circumstances will help you if and when unplanned events happen.

If players are late, you may have to adjust your starting lineup. Although this may not be a major inconvenience, you should stress to your players that there are important reasons for being on time. First, part of being a member of a team is being committed to and responsible for the other members. When players don't show up, or show up late, they break that commitment. And second, players need to go through the team warm-up to physically and mentally prepare for the game. Skipping the warm-up risks injury, and players who don't warm up may not be focused and prepared to play the game.

There may be a time when an emergency causes you to be late or miss a game. In these cases, you should notify your assistant coach, if you have one, or the league coordinator. If notified in advance, a parent of a player or another volunteer might be able to step in for the game. You should always keep a phone list with you containing the numbers of all the parents and coaches.

Sometimes a game will be postponed because of inclement weather or for other reasons, such as unsafe court conditions. If the postponement takes place before game day, you must call every member of your team to let them know. If it happens while the teams are on-site and preparing for the game, you should gather your team members and explain why the game has been postponed. Make sure that all your players have a ride home before you leave—you should be the last to leave.

During the Game

Throughout the game, you must keep the competition in proper perspective and help your players do the same. Observe how your players execute skills and how well they play together. These observations will help you decide appropriate practice plans for the following week. Let's take a more detailed look at your responsibilities during a game.

Tactical Decisions

Although you won't need to create a complex game strategy, as mentioned before, you will need to make tactical decisions in several areas throughout a game. You'll make decisions about who starts the game (and in what positions) and when to enter substitutes, about making slight adjustments to your team's tactics, about calling time-outs, and about dealing with players' performance errors.

Starting and Substituting Players

Your league should specify its rules and expectations for substituting players, and you should have your substitution plan ready before each game. When considering playing time, make sure that everyone on the team gets to play at least half of each game. This should be your guiding principle as you consider starting and substitution patterns, unless your league rules specify a different approach. You should explain your substitution plan to your players and their parents so everyone will know what to expect in the game. It is also wise to practice the substitution procedures with your players before a game.

At the youth level, the most common method of substitution is to allow a team member to enter the game to replace the person who has just rotated back to serve. This works well for younger players because it makes it easy to understand when to enter the game and whom to go in for. This method also ensures that each player gets equal playing time, because the players rotate through all the positions on the court.

Another substitution method is to pair players in each position (two players are assigned to the right-back position, two to the left-back position, and so on) and split the game in half. For example, if you're playing to 15 points, players come in to substitute for their assigned partner when one team has reached 8 points. Remember to switch this around for each game to give each player the opportunity to start a game and to ensure equal repetitions.

See "Substitutions" on page 35 of chapter 3 for more information on general substitution rules.

Adjusting Team Tactics

For players aged 11 and under (for 3v3 and 4v4 play), you probably won't adjust your team tactics too significantly during a game. Rather, you'll focus on the basic tactics, and during breaks, you'll emphasize the specific tactics your team needs to work on. However, coaches of 12- to 14-year-olds (6v6 play) might have reason to make tactical adjustments to improve their team's chances of performing well and winning. As games progress, assess your opponent's style of play and tactics, and make adjustments that are appropriate—that is, those that your players are prepared for and have learned in practice. You may want to consider the following examples when adjusting team tactics:

- Do any of the opposing team's passers fail to pay attention to the server? If so, you might want to tell your servers to serve to that player's area of the court more often.

- Does the opposing team's offense revolve around a couple of key hitters? If this is the case, you might instruct your blockers and defense to anticipate those hitters getting the majority of the sets.

- Is the opposing team's defense leaving certain areas of the court open? This might prompt you to tell your hitters to hit to certain holes in the defense.

- Does the opposing setter only set to certain hitters or spots on the court? Does she give away her intentions before she sets? You might instruct your blockers to watch the setter, anticipate where she will set, and begin to move there.

- Does the opponent block with one or two blockers on every hit? You might tell your hitters to tip over the block.

Knowing the answers to such questions can help you formulate an effective game plan and make proper adjustments during a game. However, don't stress tactics too much during a game. Doing so can take the fun out of the game for the players. You should carry a pen and pad to note which team tactics and individual skills need attention. This will help you plan out your next practice.

Correcting Players' Errors

In chapter 6, you learned about two types of errors: learning errors and performance errors. Learning errors are those that occur because players don't know how to perform a skill. Performance errors are made not because players don't know how to execute the skill, but because they make mistakes in carrying out what they do know—usually in terms of anticipation, reading, timing, or judgment.

Sometimes it's not easy to tell which type of error players are making. Knowing your players' capabilities helps you to determine if they know the skill and are simply making mistakes in executing it or if they don't know how to perform it. If they are making learning errors—that is, they don't know how to perform the skills—you should note this and cover it at the next practice. Game time is not the time to teach skills.

If they are making performance errors, however, you can help players correct those errors during a game. Players who make performance errors often do so because they have a lapse in concentration or motivation, or they are simply demonstrating human error. Competition can also adversely affect a young player's technique, and a word of encouragement about concentration may help. If you do correct a performance error during a game, do so in a quiet, controlled, and positive tone of voice during breaks in the game or when the player is on the bench with you.

> **Coaching Tip**
> Designate an area near the team bench where players gather after coming off the court during time-outs and between games. In this area, you can speak to them either individually or as a group and make necessary adjustments.

For those making performance errors, you must determine if the error is just an occasional error that anyone can make or if it is an expected error for a youngster at that stage of development. If the latter is the case, then the player may appreciate your not commenting on the mistake. The player knows it was a mistake and may already know how to correct it. On the other hand, perhaps an encouraging word and a "coaching cue" (such as "Remember to tilt your forearm platform to direct the ball to your target!") may be just what the player needs. Knowing the players and what to say is very much a part of the "art" of coaching.

Coach and Player Behavior

Another aspect of coaching on game day is managing behavior—both yours and your players'. As a coach, it is your responsibility to control emotions when aspects of the game, such as your tactics, are not working as you or your players would have hoped.

Coach Conduct

You very much influence your players' behavior before, during, and after a game. If you're up, your players are more likely to be up. If you're anxious, they'll take notice, and the anxiety can become contagious. If you're negative, they'll respond with worry. If you're positive, they'll play with more enjoyment. If you're constantly yelling instructions or commenting on mistakes and errors, it will be difficult for players to concentrate. Instead, you should let players get into the flow of the game.

The focus should be on positive competition and on having fun. A coach who overorganizes everything and dominates a game from the sideline is definitely not making the game fun. So how should you conduct yourself? Here are a few pointers:

- Be calm, in control, and supportive of your players.

- Encourage players often, but instruct during play sparingly. Players should focus on their performance during a game, not on instructions shouted from the bench. Remember that if you have to yell at your players during a game, you probably have not coached them well enough in practice.

- If you need to instruct a player, do so when you're both on the bench, in an unobtrusive manner. Never yell at players for making a mistake. Instead, briefly demonstrate or remind them of the correct technique, and encourage them. Tell them how to correct the problem on the court.

You should also make certain that you have discussed sideline demeanor as a coaching staff, and that everyone is in agreement on the way the coaches should conduct themselves on the bench. Remember, you're not playing for an Olympic gold medal! At this level, volleyball competitions are designed to help players develop their skills and themselves—and to have fun. So coach in a manner at games that helps your players achieve these things.

Player Conduct

You're responsible for keeping your players under control. Do so by setting a good example and by disciplining when necessary. Set team rules for good behavior. If players attempt to cheat, fight, argue, badger, yell disparaging remarks, and the like, it is your responsibility to correct the misbehavior. Initially, this may mean removing players immediately from the game (substituting for them), letting them calm down, and then speaking to them quietly, explaining that their behavior is not acceptable for your team—and that if they want to play, they must not repeat the action. You must remember, too, that younger players are still learning how to deal with their emotions in addition to learning the game. As a coach, you must strive to remain calm during times when young players are having trouble controlling their emotions.

You should consider team rules in these areas of game conduct:

- Player language
- Player behavior
- Interactions with officials
- Discipline for misbehavior
- Dress code for competitions

Player Welfare

All players are not the same. Some attach their self-worth to winning and losing. This idea is fueled by coaches, parents, peers, and society, who place great emphasis on winning. Players become anxious when they're uncertain whether they can meet the expectations of others—especially when meeting a particular expectation is important to them also.

If your players look uptight and anxious during a game, you should find ways to reduce both the uncertainties about how their performance will be evaluated and the importance they are attaching to the game. Help players focus on realistic personal goals—goals that are reachable and measurable and that will help them improve their performance while having fun as they play. Another way to reduce anxiety on game day is to stay away from emotional pregame pep talks. Instead, remind players of the techniques and tactics they will use, and remind them to play hard, to do their best, and to have fun. Tell them that you care more about their not letting anyone outhustle them on the court than you do about whether they win or lose.

When coaching during games, remember that the most important outcome from playing volleyball is to build or enhance players' self-worth. Keep that firmly in mind, and strive to promote this through every coaching decision.

Keeping the Game Safe

Chapter 4 is devoted to player safety, but it's worth noting here that safety during games can be affected by how officials call the rules. If officials aren't calling rules correctly and this risks injury to your players, you must intervene. Voice your concern in a respectful manner and in a way that places the emphasis where it should be—on the players' safety. One of the officials' main responsibilities is to provide for players' safety. Both you and the officials are working together to protect the players whenever possible. Don't hesitate to address an issue of safety with an official when the need arises.

Opponents and Officials

You must respect opponents and officials. Without them, there wouldn't be a competition. Opponents provide opportunities for your team to test itself, improve, and excel. Officials help provide a fair and safe experience for players and, as appropriate, help them learn the game.

You and your team should show respect for opponents and officials by giving your best efforts and being civil. Don't allow your players to "trash talk" or taunt an opponent or an official. Such behavior is disrespectful to the spirit of the competition, and you should immediately remove a player from a match (as discussed previously in "Player Conduct") if that player disobeys your team rules in this area. Remember, in volleyball only the floor captain and the coach are legally allowed to address the officials.

Remember, too, that officials at this level are quite often teenagers—in many cases not much older than the players themselves—and the level of officiating should be commensurate to the level of play. In other words, don't expect perfection from officials any more than you do from your own players. As long as the calls are being made consistently on both sides, most of your officiating concerns will be alleviated.

After the Game

When the game is over, join your team in congratulating the coaches and players of the opposing team, then be sure to thank the officials. Check on any injuries players sustained during the game, and inform players on how to care for them at home. Be prepared to speak with the officials about any problems that occurred during the game. Then, hold a brief postgame meeting (described later) to ensure that your players are on an even keel—whether they won or lost—and to focus them on the positives and the goals for the next practice or game.

Reactions Following a Game

Your first concern after a game should be your players' attitudes and mental well-being. You don't want them to be too high after a win or too low after a loss. This is the time you can be most influential in helping players keep the outcome in perspective and settle their emotions.

When celebrating a victory, make sure your team does so in a way that doesn't show disrespect for the opponents. It's okay and appropriate to be happy and celebrate a win, but don't allow your players to taunt the opponents or boast about their victory. If your team was defeated, your players will naturally be disappointed. But, if your team has made a winning effort, let them know this. After a loss, help them keep their chins up and maintain a positive attitude that will carry over into the next practice and game. Winning and losing are a part of life, not just a part of sport. If players can handle both equally well, they'll be successful in whatever they do.

Coaching Tip

Before conducting the postgame team meeting, you should lead your players through a cool-down similar to the one you use to end your practice sessions. This will not only help players improve their flexibility, but it will also help them calm down after the game so they can focus on what you are about to say. The younger the player, the shorter your postgame cool-down and team meeting should be. For players in the 6- to 9-year age group, keep the postgame routine to no more than 10 minutes; for older players, keep it to no more than 15 minutes.

Postgame Team Meeting

Following the game, gather your team in a designated area for a short meeting. Before this meeting, decide as a coaching staff what to say and who will say it. Be sure that the staff speaks with one voice following the game.

If your players have performed well in a game, you should compliment them and congratulate them. Tell them specifically what they did well, whether they won or lost. This will reinforce their desire to repeat their good performances. Don't use this time to criticize individual players for poor performances in front of teammates or attempt to go over tactical problems and adjustments. You should help players improve their skills, but do so at the next practice. Immediately after a game, players won't absorb much tactical information. Instead, you should focus on the individual and team goals for the next practice or game.

Finally, make sure your players have transportation home. Always be the last one to leave to ensure full supervision of your players.

10

Developing Season and Practice Plans

We hope you've learned a lot from this book: what your responsibilities are as a coach, how to communicate well and provide for safety, how to teach and shape skills, and how to coach on game days. But match days make up only a portion of your season—you and your players will spend more time in practices than in competition. How well you conduct practices and prepare your players for competition will greatly affect not only your players' enjoyment and success throughout the season, but also your own.

Fun Learning Environment

Regardless of what point you're at in your season, you should work to create an environment that welcomes learning and promotes teamwork. Following are seven tips to help you and your coaching staff get the most out of your practices:

1. Stick to the practice times agreed on as a staff.

2. Start and end each practice as a team.

3. Keep the practice routine as consistent as possible so the players can feel comfortable.

4. Be organized in your approach by moving quickly from one activity to another and from one stage of training to another so that time is not wasted.

5. Tell your players what the practice will include before the practice starts.

6. Allow the players to take water breaks whenever possible.

7. Focus on providing immediate, positive, and specific feedback—but make sure you don't critique every contact and move a player makes.

In addition to the drills provided throughout chapter 7 in this book, you may also want to consider using gamelike drills to add variety and make practices more fun. In appendix C, you will find 12 gamelike drills. Using gamelike drills during each practice can help prepare players for the many different situations that arise in competition. It also allows for more skill transfer from the practices into the competition.

Season Plans

Your season plan acts as a snapshot of the entire season. Before the first practice with your players, you must sit down as a coaching staff and develop such a plan. To do so, simply take a blank monthly calendar page and write down each practice and game date, then go back and number the practices. These practice numbers are the foundation of your season plan. Now you can work through the plan, moving from practice to practice, outlining what you hope to achieve in each practice. You should note the purpose of each practice; the main skills you will cover; and the activities, drills, and games you will use to achieve the goals and objectives of each practice.

Following is more detailed information about season plans for three particular age groups in youth volleyball: ages 6 to 9 (3v3 play), ages 10 to 11 (4v4 play), and ages 12 to 14 (6v6 play). Your league may use different age breakdowns—8 to 9, 10 to 11, and 12 to 14 is a common breakdown, as is 9 to 11 and 12 to 14, depending on the number of players available in your area. Some leagues will also have volleyball opportunities for players in the 6- to 7-year age group (often in the form of 3v3, which is generally played up through age 9). You may need to adjust the season plans to accommodate the skill level you are coaching—don't rely solely on the players' ages to develop your plan. For example, you might use the 6- to 9-year age group's plan for a team of 11- and 12-year-olds who are new to volleyball; conversely, if you live in an area where leagues start at age 8, you might be able to use the 12- to 14-year age group's plan for a group of experienced 10-year-olds who have already been playing volleyball for 2 years and have a good understanding of the basics. In addition, your local league may use various surfaces for play, such as indoor or outdoor hard courts or outdoor grass or sand courts, all of which may also be different for each age group (see chapter 3).

Part of the art of coaching is being able to adjust your plan if the situation warrants it. If your players are having trouble with specific skills, you might adjust your season plan to allow more practice time for those particular skills. On the other hand, if your players are bored because they've already learned the skills you're introducing, don't be afraid to adjust your plan to include teaching new skills (or advanced versions of the same skills) and strategies that increase the challenge and the players' understanding of the game.

Coaching Tip

While developing your season plan, keep in mind that you will want to incorporate the games approach into your practices. The games approach is superior to the traditional (isolated skills) approach because it focuses on replicating the game environment. Using gamelike drills better prepares the players, both physically and mentally, for the demands of the competitive game.

Season Plan for Ages 6 to 9

Many players in this age group have had little or no exposure to volleyball. Don't assume that they have any knowledge of the game. You should help them explore the basic tactics and skills of the sport, as suggested in the following season plan.

Practice	Purpose	Related skills	Related gamelike drills
1	Introduction to the game and the team; assessment and development of overhead passing skills	Moving to the ball	Setting Pretty, page 184
2	Introduction to the game; development and practice of overhead passing skills	Moving to the ball; decision making; communication	Pass to Paradise, page 185
3	Assessment and development of forearm passing skills	Moving to the ball; communication	Nail It, page 186
4	Development and practice of forearm passing skills; introduction to serve receive	Moving to the ball; decision making; communication	I Can Pass, page 189 Pinball Passes, page 187
5	Assessment and development of serving skills	Aiming or targeting a serve; passing; serve receiving	In the Zone, page 190
6	Review and practice of serving, receiving, and passing skills	Moving to the ball; decision making; communication; teamwork	In the Zone, page 190 Three for the Money, page 180
7	Review and practice of serving and serve-receiving skills	Aiming or targeting a serve; passing; serve receiving	Target Passing, page 188
8	Review and practice of forearm passing skills	Moving to the ball; pursuing the ball; communication	Pinball Passes, page 187
9	Review and practice of overhead passing (setting) skills	Performing back sets and back-row sets; executing pass, set, hit sequences	Setting Pretty, page 184 Three for the Money, page 180
10	Introduction to player positions; review and practice of passing skills	Digging attacks; team defense; team offense	Pinball Passes, page 187 Three for the Money, page 180
11	Review and practice of serving skills; scrimmage with focus on serve placement	Executing pass, set, hit sequences	In the Zone, page 190
12	Skill review and practice for combination play and positions; scrimmage	Teamwork; communication; understanding rules	Three for the Money, page 180
13	Skill practice for combination play and positions; 3v3 tournament	Teamwork; communication; understanding rules and subbing	Three for the Money, page 180
14	Skill practice for combination play and positions; scrimmage	Teamwork; communication; understanding rules, officiating, and subbing	Three for the Money, page 180

Season Plan for Ages 10 to 11

The season plan for this age group builds on the previous one (for ages 6 to 9) as players practice the fundamental tactics and skills. A few new tactics are also added, including positioning, hitting the ball, and executing the dig.

Practice	Purpose	Related skills	Related gamelike drills
1	Introduction to the team; assessment, development, and practice of overhead passing skills	Receiving free balls; setting	Pass to Paradise, page 185
2	Assessment, development, and practice of forearm passing skills	Receiving free balls; serving; serve receiving	I Can Pass, page 189
3	Assessment, development, and practice of serving skills	Overhand and jump serving; serve receiving; setting	In the Zone, page 190
4	Review and practice of serve-receive alignments and positions	Serving; serve receiving; setting	Nail It, page 186
5	Skill practice for combination play; development of tactical skills	Targeting a serve; serve receiving; setting	Three for the Money, page 180
6	Review and practice of team positioning; practice of serving, receiving, and passing skills	Serving; serve receiving	Skeet Shooting, page 182 Target Passing, page 188
7	Assessment, development, and practice of attacking skills	Digging or receiving a serve; setting	Hammer Time, page 181
8	Review and practice of hitting skills; skill practice for combination play	Digging or receiving a serve; setting; covering your hitter	Hammer Time, page 181 Target Passing, page 188
9	Review and practice of overhead passing (setting) skills	Setting; team communication	Pass to Paradise, page 185 Target Passing, page 188
10	Assessment and development of digging skills	Attacking; blocking; team defense positions	Dig 'Em High, page 191
11	Development and practice of serving skills (overhand serve)	Jump serving; serve receiving; setting; attacking; team communication	Skeet Shooting, page 182
12	Review and practice of serving skills (overhand serve); scrimmage	Jump serving; serve receiving; setting; attacking (blocking); communication; understanding rules and officiating; understanding subbing and time-out procedures	Skeet Shooting, page 182
13	Skill practice for combination play and positions; 4v4 tournament	Playing offense and defense; communication; understanding rules and officiating; understanding subbing and time-out procedures	Three for the Money, page 180
14	Skill practice for combination play and positions; scrimmage	Playing offense and defense; communication; understanding rules and officiating; understanding subbing and time-out procedures	Three for the Money, page 180

Season Plan for Ages 12 to 14

The season plan for this age group is designed to help players refine the skills they have learned in previous years. This plan builds on the previous one by adding a few new skills, including blocking and overhand jump serves.

Practice	Purpose	Related skills	Related gamelike drills
1	Introduction to the team; assessment and review of passing skills	Overhead and forearm passing; receiving free balls	Pass to Paradise, page 185 Target Passing, page 188
2	Assessment and review of hitting skills	Setting; blocking; digging	Hammer Time, page 181
3	Assessment and review of serving skills	Passing; serve receiving	Skeet Shooting, page 182
4	Review and practice of serve-reception skills	Serving; setting; targeting; communication; decision making	Nail It, page 186
5	Review and practice of hitting skills	Setting; blocking; digging	Hammer Time, page 181
6	Assessment and development of blocking skills	Hitting; digging	Block-Out, page 192
7	Review of strategies for combination play	Executing serve, pass, hit, block sequences	Three for the Money, page 180
8	Review of team positioning	Receiving free balls; serve receiving; playing defense; attacking	In the Zone, page 190 Three for the Money, page 180
9	Assessment and review of digging skills	Attacking; blocking	Dig 'Em High, page 191
10	Review and practice of digging skills	Attacking; blocking; positioning for team defense	Dig 'Em High, page 191 Hammer Time, page 181
11	Review and practice of serving skills	Targeting; passing; setting; attacking; serve-receive positioning; communication	In the Zone, page 190
12	Review and practice of serving skills; scrimmage	Targeting; passing; setting; attacking; serve-receive positioning; communication	In the Zone, page 190
13	Skill practice for combination play and positions; 6v6 tournament	Serving; passing; setting; attacking; blocking; digging; serve-receive positioning; communication; understanding rules and officiating; understanding time-out procedures	Three for the Money, page 180
14	Skill practice for combination play and positions; scrimmage	Serving; passing; setting; attacking; blocking; digging; serve-receive positioning; communication; understanding rules and officiating; understanding time-out procedures	Three for the Money, page 180

Practice Plans

Coaches rarely believe they have enough time to practice everything they want to cover. To help organize your thoughts and help you stay on track toward your practice objectives, you should create written practice plans. These plans help you better visualize and prepare so you can run your practices effectively.

First, your practice plans should be appropriate for the age group and skill level of the players you are coaching. The plans should incorporate all the skills and concepts presented in that particular age group's season plan. To begin, each practice plan should note the practice objective (which is drawn from your season plan) as well as the equipment and court space necessary to execute the specific activities in the practice. Each practice plan should also include a warm-up and cool-down. The cool-down should include postpractice stretching, and coaches should attend to any injuries suffered during practice and make sure the players drink plenty of water.

Sample Practice Plan for Ages 6 to 9

Objective
Get to know teammates and coaches; evaluation of overhead passing; teach and practice overhead passing

Equipment
One or two courts with antennae; at least one ball per player; ball buckets or baskets; visible score device

Activity	Description	Coaching points
Prepractice meeting (5 min.)	The coach takes roll call. The coach explains the purpose of the practice: to introduce overhead passing and to allow players to get to know one another (by playing a "name game" or other icebreaker activity).	• Make eye contact with every player • Practice remembering each player's name and something about each player
Warm-up (10 min.)	Players line up along the end line. While in a defensive ready stance, the players make five trips from the end line to the net and back, in the following sequence: 1. Jog slowly 2. Slide slowly facing the right sideline 3. Slide slowly facing the left sideline 4. Zigzag facing the net 5. Take lunge steps slowly, alternating legs	• Warming up the muscles • Learning basic volleyball movement patterns on the court • Improving agility and balance • Preparing muscles for ballhandling and pursuit of the ball

(continued)

Activity	Description	Coaching points
Overhead passing skills: introduction (10 min.)	Coaches demonstrate the whole skill of overhead passing from at least two angles with proper cues (three or four cues). Players practice with a partner or in groups of three, and coaches observe players' current skill level. Next, players gather, and the coaches again demonstrate (and give cues) on overhead passing—this time with a focus on the feet and knees; players then practice with partners or in groups, with the coaches circulating among players and reinforcing cues, correcting, demonstrating, and praising. Repeat with the focus on the hand and arm position, extension, and follow-through.	• Catch players "doing it right" • Using overhand passing action • Keeping feet staggered and balanced with knees bent • Forming ball-shaped "window" above forehead • Following through high to target
Overhead passing skills (5 min.)	Practice overhead passing with a coach (or player) on one side of the net and three players on the other side—one in the right-back (RB) passing position, one at the setter's position near the attack line, and one in the left-front (LF) hitting position. The coach makes the first overhead pass over the net to the RB player, who passes the ball to the player in the setting position using an overhead pass; the setter overhead passes to the LF player, who overhead passes back over the net to the coach to begin the sequence again. After a specified number of repetitions (or successful repetitions, or time period), players rotate one position and repeat the drill.	• Facing the target • Raising hands above the forehead • Extending high • Executing three-hit sequences
Overhead passing skills (10 min.)	Practice overhead passing by dividing players into two lines, with the first player in each line in the LB, and RF positions. A coach (or player) will toss the ball over the net (progressing to serving) to the LB to initiate play. The LB overhead passes to the RF and then moves to follow into hitter coverage and joins that line (the RF line). The RF catches the ball and moves to the passing line (the LB line).	• Passing high balls to your attackers' corners of the court • Calling the ball

Activity	Description	Coaching points
Overhead passing skills (10 min.)	Practice overhead passing using the same formation and passing sequence as in the previous drill, except passers now pass to the setter, who is positioned 3 meters off the net, but near the center of the net. The setter alternates overhead passes to the right-front (RF) and left-front (LF) players. The RF or LF player overhead passes over the net to a coach or a catcher. Skilled players may be able to keep the ball going in the air and over the net without stopping to enter a new ball into the drill sequence.	• Getting into position and facing the target • Calling the ball • Passing high, settable balls
Overhead passing skills (5-10 min.)	Practice overhead passing to the hitter using the same formation and passing sequence as in the previous drill, where the setter passes (sets) the ball to the RF and LF players. However, the RF or LF player should now make the third contact over the net using a tip or off-speed shot. The setter sets three overhead passes to both the RF and LF player; rotate players so that all players have a chance as the setter and as the hitters.	• Setting 3 meters or more off the net • Passing 3 meters or more off the net
Game: Three for the Money (20 min.)	Play Three for the Money as described on page 180 to stress proper overhead passing technique. Teams of three (or four) players will score points for returning the ball across the net with a pass, set, hit sequence in which at least one contact is an overhead pass.	• Calling the ball early • Moving quickly to the ball • Getting into position and facing the target • Passing high, settable balls • Emphasize teamwork

(continued)

Sample Practice Plan for Ages 6 to 9 *(continued)*

Activity	Description	Coaching points
Cool-down (5 min.)	Play Queen of the Court versus the coach. An overhead pass is the only skill that counts for points; players must complete a three-pass sequence over the net back to the coach to win a point. Teams stay on for another ball from the coach as long as they complete the required sequence; teams rotate off if they fail to complete the required sequence, and a new team then gets the chance to score. Play short games of first team to 5 or 7 points. After 5 minutes of play, the coach should lead the players in static stretching.	• Lowering heart rate and body temperature • Repetition of the overhead pass position • Goal setting
Team meeting (5 min.)	Review positives from the practice; discuss goals for the next practice.	• Make eye contact with each player • Mention players by name who made improvements

Sample Practice Plan for Ages 10 to 11

Objective

Review of passing and serving skills; practice combinations of skills with different combinations of players on the court; serving and serve-receiving strategies, specifically serving to open zones, passing settable balls, and setting the correct hitter based on the pass quality

Equipment

One or two courts with antennae; at least one ball for each player; one or two ball buckets; flat and upright targets

Activity	Description	Coaching points
Prepractice meeting (5 min.)	The coach takes roll call, reviews the positive aspects of the previous practice, and explains the purpose of today's practice: serving smart and serve receiving consistently to score.	• Make eye contact with every player • Single out good performances • Mention players by name who improved in previous day's work • Continue getting to know each other
Warm-up (20 min.)	Players line up along the end line. While in a defensive ready position, the players make five trips from the end line to the net and back, in the following sequence: 1. Jog slowly 2. Slide slowly facing the right sideline 3. Slide slowly facing the left sideline 4. Zigzag facing the net 5. Take lunge steps slowly, alternating legs Players then line up on either side of the net and warm up the arms by throwing over the net. They begin with two-hand overhead throws and progress to one-hand overhead throws; they finish by making forearm and overhead passes over the net.	• Increasing circulation • Loosening muscles • Improving movement skills • Preparing for ball handling, serving, and pursuit of balls
Game: Pass to Paradise (15 min.)	Play Pass to Paradise as described on page 185, but award points only for successful forearm passes rather than overhead passes. Points are awarded only for attacks initiated by successful forearm passes to the setter. Alternate tosses between teams, regardless of which team wins the rally. Rotate players after each rally. Freeze play and comment when necessary.	• Combining sequences of skills in gamelike situations • Working on communication and decision making with one or two other players

(continued)

Sample Practice Plan for Ages 10 to 11 *(continued)*

Activity	Description	Coaching points
Game: Nail It (20 min.)	Play Nail It as described on page 186. Freeze play and comment when necessary.	• Combining sequences of skills in gamelike situations • Working on communication and decision making • Serving to weaker zones or passers • Passing settable balls
Game: Nail It (20 min.)	Play Nail It as described on page 186, but in each rotation, place receivers in the serve-receive alignments you will use during the next game.	• Serving to weaker zones or passers • Working on communication and decision making • Passing settable balls from specific serve-receive alignments
Game: Queen of the Court (15 min.)	Play 2v2, 3v3, or 4v4 Queen of the "Mississippi" Court, where winners of the rally stay on and assume (or maintain) positions on the "queen's side" of the court. The team that does not win the rally rotates out, and a new "challenging" team enters. The challenging team gets to serve to the winner's side after they count off "one Mississippi, two Mississippi," and so on (the coach can designate any number of "Mississippis"). This forces the winning team to hustle under the net when running to the queen's side, or if already there, they must rotate quickly before the serve arrives. Play to a designated number of points; when one team reaches that score, the game is over.	• Working on communication and teamwork during serve receive • Using good judgment when setting • Executing three-hit passing sequences • Serving to specific targets • Assuming positions in serve-receive alignment quickly to be ready to receive serve
Cool-down (5 min.)	Play In the Zone as described on page 190. After the game, the coach should lead static stretching. Players can then pair up to give each other back massages using the ball (one player lies on her belly while her partner rolls the volleyball around on her shoulders, back, and legs).	• Lowering heart rate and body temperature • Improving consistency in serving to specific targets or zones • Relaxing the muscles
Team meeting (5 min.)	Review positives from the practice; discuss goals for the next practice.	• Make eye contact with each player • Mention players by name who made improvements

Sample Practice Plan for Ages 12 to 14

Objective

Review and practice overhand floater, topspin, and jump serves; serving from additional zones of the end line; serving aggressively to targets; using advanced serves in a scrimmage situation

Equipment

One or two courts with antennae; at least one ball for each player; one or two ball buckets; flat and upright targets

Activity	Description	Coaching points
Prepractice meeting (5 min.)	The coach takes roll call, reviews the positives from the previous practice, and explains the purpose of today's practice: working on aggressive serving to targets, serving strategy for the game (specifically, the jump serves), and team building.	• Make eye contact with every player • Single out good performances • Mention players by name who improved in previous day's work
Warm-up (15 min.)	Players line up along the end line. While in a defensive ready position, the players make five trips from the end line to the net and back, in the following sequence: 1. Jog slowly 2. Slide slowly facing the right sideline 3. Slide slowly facing the left sideline 4. Zigzag facing the net 5. Take lunge steps slowly, alternating legs Players then line up on either side of the net from sideline to sideline near the attack line. Players partner up to play 1v1, then 2v2, then 3v3 over-the-net pepper in the short court. Divide the net into two or three courts that use the attack line as the end line. In 1v1, each player gets three contacts to put the ball over the net to her partner, beginning with three forearm passes; then three overhead passes; then a pass, set, tip (or off-speed hit) sequence. Once players are warm, they may jump and tip (or off-speed hit) over the net on the third contact. The same sequence is followed when playing 2v2 or 3v3.	• Increasing circulation • Loosening muscles • Improving reading, anticipation, timing, and judgment • Preparing for ball-handling, attacking, and pursuit of balls

(continued)

Sample Practice Plan for Ages 12 to 14 *(continued)*

Activity	Description	Coaching points
Serving skills (15 min.)	Players perform a serving drill where they pair up and serve over the net using a self-toss, jump, and swing (jump serve). They start from the attack line and gradually increase their distance until they are serving from the end line. After each serve from the end line, players must run onto the court to simulate a defensive dig, then get into ready position to receive their partner's serve. Whenever possible, the passer then passes the served ball up to herself, catches it, and runs to the end line to serve to her partner again.	• Making good tosses • Using proper footwork on the approach • Using proper movement of hitting arm • Following through to target • Practicing action and movement after serving
Game: In the Zone (15 min.)	Play In the Zone as described on page 190 to practice serving and serve receiving. Divide players into two groups (servers and passers).	• Assuming passing formations for serve receiving • Transitioning to attack after a serve • Serving into open zones or into seams of the serve-receive formation • Covering the seams
Serving and serve-receiving skills (20 min.)	Players perform a 3v3 or 4v4 "wash" drill to practice serving and serve receiving. One team must win two rallies in a row to score a point. If one team wins a rally and the other team wins the second rally, it is a "wash" and no points are scored for winning those rallies. A new ball is initiated by the serving team; serves are alternated, so each team must win a served and a received ball to score a point. Award one bonus point for all jump serve attempts and two bonus points for successful jump serves (even if the team doesn't win the rally). A team that wins the two "wash" rallies is awarded one additional point.	• Encouraging players to attempt a jump serve in a competitive game • Focusing on winning several rallies in a row

Activity	Description	Coaching points
Game: Nail It (15 min.)	Play Nail It as described on page 186. Require servers to serve into specific zones or seams between zones, or to call the zone they will serve into. Award bonus points for serving where they call.	• Serving into open zones or into seams of the serve-receive formation • Practicing aggressive serving • Covering the seams • Reading the server's intentions and the trajectory of the ball
Controlled scrimmage (15 min.)	Play a modified scrimmage game using full teams on a competitive court. The receiving team should use their serve-receive alignments for each rotation. Require servers to identify zones they will serve into. Coaches should freeze and shape play as necessary.	• Serving into specific zones or into seams of the serve-receive formation • Practicing aggressive serving • Covering the seams • Reading the server's intentions and the trajectory of the ball
Cool-down (5 min.)	Players play an over-the-net pepper game in the short court. They pass back and forth over the net in teams of two or three, using three contacts per side, but no jumping (using only overhand passes, roll shots, tips on the third contact). After the game, the coach should lead static stretching. Players can then pair up to give each other back massages using the ball.	• Lowering heart rate and body temperature • Using proper form for passes and hits over the net
Team meeting (5 min.)	Review positives from the practice; discuss goals for the next practice.	• Make eye contact with each player • Mention players by name who made improvements

Constructing practice plans requires both organization and flexibility on your part. Don't be intimidated by the amount of material you've listed in your season plan as skills and tactics you want to cover. Pick out a few basics and build your initial practice plans around them; this process will get easier after you've drafted a few plans. Then you can move from teaching simple concepts and skills to drawing up plans that introduce more complex ones. Build in some flexibility; if you find that what you've planned for practice isn't working, you should have a backup activity planned that approaches the skill or concept from a slightly different angle. The top priorities are to keep your team playing the game and to help everyone have fun while they're learning.

Appendix A

Related Checklists and Forms

This appendix contains checklists and forms that will be useful in your volleyball program. All checklists and forms mentioned in the text can be found here. You may reproduce and use these checklists and forms as needed for your volleyball program.

Facilities and Equipment Checklist

Facility

❑ The stairs and corridors leading to the gym are well lit.

❑ The stairs and corridors are free of obstruction.

❑ The stairs and corridors are in good repair.

❑ Exits are well marked and illuminated.

❑ Exits are free of obstruction and are unlocked from the inside.

❑ Uprights, referee stands, and other projections are padded.

❑ Walls are free of projections (or padded if present).

❑ Windows are located high on the walls.

❑ Wall plugs and light switches are insulated and protected.

❑ Lights are shielded.

❑ Lighting is sufficient to illuminate the playing area well.

❑ The heating and cooling system for the gym is working properly and is monitored regularly.

❑ Ducts, radiators, pipes, and so on are shielded or designed to withstand high impact.

❑ Tamper-free thermostats are housed in impact-resistant covers.

❑ The track has secure railings with a minimum height of three feet, six inches.

❑ The track has direction signs posted.

❑ The track is free of obstructions.

❑ Rules for the track are posted.

❑ Projections on the track are padded or illuminated.

From ASEP, 2007, *Coaching youth volleyball*, 4th ed. (Champaign, IL: Human Kinetics).

❑ Gym equipment is inspected before and during each use.

❑ The gym is adequately supervised.

❑ Galleries and viewing areas have been designed to protect small children by blocking their access to the playing area.

❑ The gym (floor, roof, walls, light fixtures, and so on) is inspected on an annual basis for safety and structural deficiencies.

❑ Fire alarms are in good working order.

❑ Fire extinguishers are up-to-date, with note of last inspection.

❑ Directions are posted for evacuating the gym in case of fire or other disaster.

Equipment

❑ Standards are stored safely and securely.

❑ Standards and floor sleeves or other connectors are in good working order.

❑ Standards, guy wires, and referee platforms are adequately padded.

❑ The net is stored safely and securely.

❑ The net is in good working order.

❑ Net cables are in good condition and not frayed or loose.

❑ Antennae are in good working order with no sharp edges or protrusions.

❑ Ball containers are provided in adequate numbers and are in good working order.

❑ Balls are stored safely, are in good condition, and are inflated properly.

❑ Score tables are in good condition with no sharp edges.

❑ Score tables are located the proper distance outside the court.

From ASEP, 2007, *Coaching youth volleyball*, 4th ed. (Champaign, IL: Human Kinetics).

Informed Consent Form

I hereby give my permission for _____ to participate in _____ during the athletic season beginning on _____. Further, I authorize the school, league, or club to provide emergency treatment of any injury or illness my child may experience if qualified medical personnel consider treatment necessary and perform the treatment. This authorization is granted only if I cannot be reached and reasonable effort has been made to do so.

Parent or guardian: _____

Address: _____

Phone: ( ) _____ **Other phone:** ( ) _____

Additional contact in case of emergency: _____

Relationship to player: _____ **Phone:** ( ) _____

Family physician: _____ **Phone:** ( ) _____

Medical conditions (e.g., allergies, chronic illness): _____

_____

_____

_____

_____

_____

_____

_____

My child and I are aware that participating in _____ is a potentially hazardous activity. We assume all risks associated with participation in this sport, including but not limited to falls, contact with other participants, the effects of the weather or traffic, and other reasonable-risk conditions associated with the sport. All such risks to my child are known and appreciated by my child and me.

We understand this informed consent form and agree to its conditions.

Player's signature: _____ **Date:** _____

Parent's or guardian's signature: _____ **Date:** _____

From ASEP, 2007, *Coaching youth volleyball*, 4th ed. (Champaign, IL: Human Kinetics).

Injury Report Form

Date of injury: _____ Time: _____ a.m./p.m.

Location: _____

Player's name: _____

Age: _____ Date of birth: _____

Type of injury: _____

Anatomical area involved: _____

Cause of injury: _____

_____

_____

Extent of injury: _____

_____

_____

Person administering first aid (name): _____

First aid administered: _____

_____

Other treatment administered: _____

_____

Referral action: _____

_____

_____

Signature of person administering first aid: _____

Date: _____

From ASEP, 2007, *Coaching youth volleyball*, 4th ed. (Champaign, IL: Human Kinetics).

Emergency Information Card

Player's name: _____

Date of birth: _____

Address: _____

Phone: (   ) _____

Provide information for parent or guardian and one additional contact in case of emergency.

Parent's or guardian's name: _____

Address: _____

Phone: (   ) _____ Other phone: (   ) _____

Additional contact's name: _____

Relationship to player: _____

Address: _____

Phone: (   ) _____ Other phone: (   ) _____

Insurance Information

Name of insurance company: _____

Policy name and number: _____

Medical Information

Physician's name: _____

Phone: (   ) _____

Is your child allergic to any drugs?   *YES   NO*

If so, what? _____

Does your child have other allergies (e.g., bee stings, dust)? _____

_____

Does your child have any of the following?   *asthma   diabetes   epilepsy*

Is your child currently taking medication?   *YES   NO*

If so, what? _____

Does your child wear contact lenses?   *YES   NO*

Is there additional information we should know about your child's health or physical condition?   *YES   NO*

If yes, please explain: _____

_____

_____

Parent's or guardian's signature: _____

Date: _____

From ASEP, 2007, *Coaching youth volleyball*, 4th ed. (Champaign, IL: Human Kinetics).

Emergency Response Card

Be prepared to give the following information to an EMS dispatcher. (*Note:* Do not hang up first. Let the EMS dispatcher hang up first.)

Caller's name: _____

Telephone number from which call is being made: _____

Reason for call: _____

How many people are injured: _____

Condition of victim(s): _____

First aid being given: _____

Location: _____

Address: _____

City: _____

Directions (e.g., cross streets, landmarks, entrance access):

From ASEP, 2007, *Coaching youth volleyball*, 4th ed. (Champaign, IL: Human Kinetics).

Appendix B

Volleyball Terms

ace—A serve that scores an immediate point (a serve that the receiving team is unable to pass).

antennae—The vertical rods attached to the net over the sidelines of the court. The antennae extend three feet above the net, and the ball must pass completely inside the antennae when it crosses the net in order to be in play. If the ball hits the antennae or crosses the net outside of them, the play is over.

approach—The movement of the attacker—usually three or four quick running steps—to get in position to jump and hit the ball.

assist—A set or pass to an attacker that leads to an immediate point.

attack—The offensive team's attempt to hit or spike the ball down into the opponent's court. The attacker's goal is to hit the ball to the floor on the opponent's side of the net to win the rally.

attacker—The player who is attempting to hit the ball down into the opponent's court to win the rally. Also called the *hitter* or *spiker*.

attack line—A line on the court 3 meters from and parallel to the net on each side that separates the frontcourt from the backcourt. Back-row players are not allowed to jump and attack the ball from in front of the attack line. Also called the *10-foot line* or the *3-meter line*.

backcourt—The area between the attack line and the end line (from sideline to sideline) on each side of the net.

baseline—The line that marks the end of the court on each side of the net. On a regulation court, each baseline is 30 feet (9 meters) from the net and runs parallel to the net. Also called the *end line*.

block—The defensive team's attempt to stop or slow down the opponent's attack at the net. A block may involve one, two, or three players getting in front of the attacker and raising their hands higher than the top of the net.

blockers—The defenders who are trying to stop or slow down the opponent's attack at the net.

centerline—A line that runs parallel to and directly under the net from sideline to sideline, dividing the court in half.

contact of the ball—A touch of the ball by any part of the player's body (except the player's loose hair).

crosscourt—The direction in which many attacks are hit—from a corner of the attacker's side of the net toward the opposite sideline or toward the diagonal corner of the opponent's side.

dig—A technique used by a defender to keep a hard-hit or tipped ball up and playable when the defender has little time to react and position herself. The defender will usually use a forearm pass or a variation of this pass to dig the ball.

double contact—When one player contacts the ball more than once with no other player touching it between these contacts. This is only legal if the player's first contact of the ball is a block.

down ball—A hit that is not a hard-driven attack or a free ball. This may include a hit made from a standing position (rather than jumping) anywhere on the court to place the ball into the opponent's court. Also called a *standing spike*.

down the line—An attack where the ball is hit from the attacker's sideline and travels straight along the opponent's same sideline.

end line—The line that marks the end of the court on each side of the net. Each end line is 30 feet (9 meters) from the net and runs parallel to the net. Also called the *baseline*.

error—A mistake that leads to a point for the opposing team. Players may make different types of errors during a game, such as a service error, ballhandling error, hitting error, receiving error, or blocking error.

float serve—A serve that floats across the net with no spin on the ball (like a knuckleball). To execute a float serve, the player makes solid contact using a "punching" action with little or no follow-through.

forearm pass—A pass in which the player uses her forearms to contact a ball arriving below her waist.

foul—Occurs when a player fails to play by the rules. You should consult your league for information on fouls and their penalties.

foot fault—Server stepping on or over the end line before contacting the serve.

free ball—A ball that is not forcefully attacked over the net, but is instead sent over using a forearm or overhead pass. Free balls are usually hit high, soft, and deep, which makes it easier for the team to counterattack.

frontcourt—The area between the net and the attack line (from sideline to sideline) on each side of the net.

held ball—A violation that occurs when the ball momentarily comes to rest in the hands or on the arms of a player during contact.

hit—The primary skill that an offensive player uses to play the ball over the net. Also called a *spike* or an *attack*.

hitter—The player who hits the ball over the net into the opponent's court. Also called a *spiker* or *attacker*.

jump serve—A serve in which the server jumps into the air (similar to an attack at the net) to contact the tossed ball.

let serve—A serve where the ball hits the net but still crosses over to the opposite side of the net.

libero—A player who is considered a back-row specialist. This player only plays in the back row and is allowed unlimited substitution into the game for any back-row player on a dead ball. The libero may not serve, set the ball to a hitter from in front of the attack line, or attack the ball from above the top of the net.

lift—A violation (illegal contact) that results when a player holds the ball.

lineup—A listing of a team's players in the positions that they will start the game in. The lineup determines the rotation of players, or the serving order, throughout the game.

live ball—A ball is considered live when it is in play—that is, from the time it is legally contacted on the serve until the rally ends and the ball is declared a dead ball.

loss of rally—A penalty assessed when the serving team violates a rule. The opponent is awarded the serve and a point.

match—A series of games—usually three or five games—played to determine the winner of the competition. The team that wins two out of three or three out of five games is the winner of the match.

net—The equipment that divides the court in half and separates the playing areas for the two teams.

off-speed attack—An attack in which the hitter attempts to deceive the defense by hitting the ball softer so that it moves slower than a hard-driven spike.

out of bounds—The area outside of the court boundaries. A ball is considered out of bounds (and becomes a dead ball) when it lands or strikes an object out of bounds.

overhead pass—A pass in which the player contacts the ball with two hands above the head.

overlap—A foul that is called when players are not in the proper serving order and alignment—with no overlapping of adjacent players (either back to front or side to side)—when the ball is served.

pass—A play in which the player contacts the ball and directs it into the air so a teammate can get into position to make the next contact.

penalty—The consequence that is applied to the offending person or team for committing an infraction of the rules.

penalty point—A point that is awarded to a team when the opposing team commits an infraction of the rules. Also called a *red card*.

penetration—The act of reaching across the net and breaking the plane of the net while blocking an attack.

pepper—A drill where players pass, set, and hit the ball back and forth to each other. Often used as a warm-up drill.

perimeter—A type of defense used to defend the areas close to the boundaries of the court.

platform—The flat surface formed by the player's forearms when executing a forearm pass. The hands should be placed together, with the thumbs and wrists pressed together. The arms should be relaxed and extended in front of the body, maintaining an even surface with the forearms to help ensure that the ball rebounds to the target.

posture—A player's body position during the execution of a skill.

rally—A sequence of continuous play back and forth across the net that begins with the serve and ends when the ball is declared a dead ball.

rally scoring—The scoring method in which a point is scored on each rally, regardless of which team served.

read—Anticipating what will occur on the court. For example, blockers will watch the setter for cues to help them anticipate where the setter will set the ball.

ready position—The position a player should assume when preparing to play the ball such as when serving, setting, attacking, receiving a pass or a dig, or blocking.

red card—The signal shown as a result of an individual or team infraction which results in a point for the opponent.

replacement—Refers to the libero player coming into the game to replace any back-row player for defensive purposes.

replay—The act of playing a rally over again—such as when a double fault occurs—without awarding a point or loss of rally and without a rotation for the serve (the same server will serve the ball again).

re-serve—Occurs when a server is allowed to serve after a tossing error. In most youth leagues, a player is allowed one service tossing error (letting the ball bounce or catching it after tossing it up for a serve) per serve attempt or per rotation—that is, the player is still allowed to serve after this occurs.

roll shot—An off-speed hit in which the player contacts the ball softly, with slow topspin, directing it to an open area of the court. Also called an *off-speed spike*.

roster—A list of all the eligible players (names and numbers) on a team.

rotate—Refers to players moving one position clockwise when their team is awarded the serve following a service by the opponent.

rotational order—The team lineup submitted before each game that identifies the players' starting positions and determines the rotation of players throughout the game. This lineup helps the scorekeeper and referee know the sequence in which players serve and verify that players are in the correct rotational order before each serve.

screening—An illegal action that involves one or more players on the serving team trying to prevent receivers from seeing the server making the serve or the path of the served ball. This could include waving arms, jumping, or moving sideways to hide the server.

seam—The area of the court between two players.

serve—The contact with the ball that initiates play to begin each rally.

server—The player who makes the initial contact to put the ball in play and begin the rally.

service error—An error made by the server while serving, such as serving a ball that fails to clear the net, serving a ball that lands out of bounds, or committing a foot fault.

set—A pass (usually a two-handed overhead pass) used to deliver the ball to an attacker.

setter—The player who makes the second contact and delivers the ball to a hitter.

sideline—The lines that mark the sides of each playing area. These lines are 30 feet (9 meters) long from the net to the end lines on each side of the net.

side-out—Occurs when the receiving team earns the right to serve by winning the rally.

spike—A forceful, hard-driven hit used to return the ball into the opponent's court.

substitution—One player entering the game to replace another player.

switch—Two teammates who change positions on the court immediately following the serve for offensive or defensive purposes. This may also refer to opposing teams that switch sides of the net at the end of each game or at the mid-point of the deciding game of the match.

tip—An attack in which the hitter uses one hand to try to softly place the ball over the blockers or into other open areas of the opponent's court.

topspin—A forward spin that can be put on the ball when attacking or serving. Topspin causes the ball to suddenly drop.

touch—A contact on the ball by a player.

transition—A team's switch from defense to offense or from offense to defense during play. May also refer to one player switching from an offensive position to a defensive position or vice versa.

underhand serve—A serve in which the server uses an underhand motion to contact the ball at waist height.

unnecessary delay—A delay in the start or resumption of a game that is caused by the action of a team, player, or coach. A first offense during a match will result in a warning. The second or subsequent offense during the same match will result in a penalty point awarded to the opponent.

USA Volleyball (USAV)—The organization that serves as the national governing body for volleyball in the United States.

warning—When an official gives notice for a first minor offense by displaying a yellow card. The warning is recorded in the scorebook, but no penalty is assessed. Also called a *yellow card*.

yellow card—Signal shown for a warning.

12 Gamelike Drills

In this appendix, you will find 12 gamelike drills that may be used in your volleyball program. These drills differ from those found in chapter 7 because they focus on creating gamelike scenarios and setting up scoring situations. As a youth volleyball coach, you can use gamelike drills during practices to keep motivation high and to make the sport fun.

Three for the Money

Goal

To use a three-hit attack to hit the ball over the net.

Description

Play 3v3 or 4v4 on a court appropriately sized for the age group of your players. To begin, a player on team A serves the ball to team B. The receiving team (B) must use a three-hit attack (pass, set, spike) and send the ball back over the net; if successful, they are awarded three points (the "money"). Play continues until the ball touches the ground, with three points being awarded for each three-hit attack. One point is also awarded to the team that wins the rally. For example, if team A wins the rally, plus successfully completes a three-hit attack, then they are awarded a total of four points. If team B did not win the rally but successfully completed a three-hit sequence, they would score three points, and the score of the game would be 4-3 after the first rally. Alternate serves between teams, regardless of which team wins the rally. Rotate players or teams after each rally.

Variations

To make the game easier for younger or less skilled players, do any of the following:

- Have the coach hit easy serves or have players toss the ball to initiate the rally.
- Require all three hits to be forearm or overhand passes.
- Award points for any three hits where the ball clears the net.
- Award extra points for a three-hit sequence that ends with an overhand attack, even if the third hit does not clear the net or goes out of bounds.
- Play 5v5.

To make the game more challenging for older or more skilled players, do any of the following:

- Only award the three points if the ball stays in the court after the three hits, or only if the final contact over the net is an overhand attack.
- Play 2v2.
- Use a different colored or marked ball as the "money ball." When this ball is in play, all points earned are doubled.
- Allow the winners to stay on the court and play a new team of players after the rotation.

Hammer Time

Goal

To score points using spikes.

Description

Play 3v3 or 4v4 on a court appropriately sized for the age group of your players. To begin, a player on team A serves the ball to team B. The receiving team (B) must use a three-hit attack (pass, set, spike), and points are awarded when the ball is spiked. One point is awarded for any attack attempt; no extra points are awarded if the ball is spiked into the net (i.e., bad mistake); one extra point is awarded if the attack goes over the net but goes out of bounds (i.e., good mistake); two points are awarded if the ball is spiked and stays in play; and three points are awarded if the ball is spiked and ends the rally. Play continues until the ball touches the ground, and an additional point is awarded to the team that wins the rally. Alternate serves between teams, regardless of which team wins the rally. Rotate players after each rally. Note that this game can also be used to focus on other types of attacks, such as off-speed hits, tips, or hitting crosscourt and down the line.

Variations

- To make the game easier for younger or less skilled players, have a coach or player initiate the rally with a toss over the net; lower the net; or play 5v5 or 6v6.
- To make the game more challenging for older or more skilled players, award points only for spikes that end a rally; award points only for a specified type of hit (tip, off speed, or hard driven); or award points only for hits that land in specified target areas of the court (crosscourt, deep middle, or line shots).

Skeet Shooting

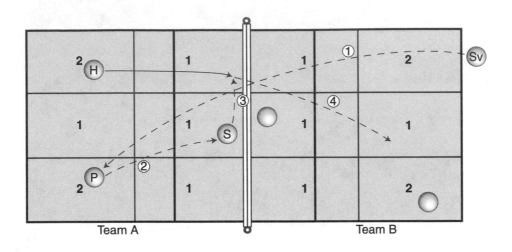

Team A   Team B

Goal

To increase hitting accuracy.

Description

Play 3v3 or 4v4 on a court appropriately sized for the age group of your players. Divide each half of the court into six zones, as shown in the diagram (the front zones and the center back zone are each worth one point; the back corner zones are each worth two points). Team B begins the game by serving or tossing the ball to team A. A player on team A (P) receives the serve and passes to the setter (S), who then sets to a hitter (H). The hitter must hit the ball over the net and into one of the marked zones using the specified skill (tip, hard-driven spike, off-speed spike, or down ball). When a player hits a ball into a zone, the designated points for that zone are awarded. Allow players to use overhead passes or forearm passes to get the ball over the net to keep the ball in play, but award points only when balls are overhand attacked to the other side. Alternate serves or tosses between teams, regardless of which team wins the rally. Rotate players after each rally or a specified series of rallies.

Variations

To make the game easier for younger or less skilled players, do any of the following:

- Make the court larger or lower the net.
- Have a coach or player toss the ball directly to the setter to begin the rally.

To make the game more challenging for older or more skilled players, do any of the following:

- Require a specified hitting technique to be used.
- Ask players to call their hits.
- Award points only if the ball hits the floor in the target zone.
- Divide the court into nine zones (front zones and back corner zones are worth three points; middle side and back center zones are worth two points; the center zone is worth one point).
- Require a certain type of hit into a certain zone to score.

Setting Pretty

Goal

To set up an attack using overhead passes.

Description

Play 3v3 or 4v4 on a court appropriately sized for the age group of your players. To begin, a player on team A serves the ball to team B. Using a three-hit attack (pass, set, hit), the receiving team (B) sends the ball back over the net. Teams are awarded two points for successful overhead passes (sets) to any hitter. Play is continuous until the rally ends. One point is also awarded to the winner of the rally. Alternate serves between teams, regardless of which team wins the rally. Rotate players after each rally.

Variations

- To make the game easier for younger or less skilled players, play 5v5; have a coach serve or toss the first ball into the rally; or award a bonus point if the overhead pass (set) to the attacker results in an attack over the net, or if the first contact is an overhead pass to the setter.
- To make the game more challenging for older or more skilled players, play 2v2; award a point only if the set results in a successful attack over the net; or award extra points for an overhead pass on the first contact that results in a successful attack.

Pass to Paradise

Goal

To set up an attack using overhead passes.

Description

Play 3v3 or 4v4 on a court appropriately sized for the age group of your players. To begin, a player on team A tosses or passes the ball over the net to initiate the rally. Points are awarded only for attacks made from overhead passes (sets) to the hitters. One point is awarded for attacks that go out of bounds; two points are awarded for attacks that stay in bounds but are returned; and three points are awarded for attacks that are in bounds and touch the floor or ground. Alternate tosses between teams, regardless of which team wins the rally. Rotate players after each rally.

Variations

- To make the game easier for younger or less skilled players, award points for overhead passes over the net on the third contact (forearm passes over the net may be used to keep the ball in play, but no points are scored).
- To make the game more challenging for older or more skilled players, play 2v2; require that the first and second contacts be overhead passes to score on the attack; or rotate positions each time the ball passes over the net to the other team.

Nail It

Goal

To make accurate forearm passes to the setter.

Description

Play 3v3 or 4v4 on a court appropriately sized for the age group of your players. To begin, a player on team A serves to initiate the rally. Players on team B use a forearm pass to receive the serve and pass the ball to a position where a teammate can use an overhead pass to set to a hitter. Three points are awarded each time a team passes the ball ("nails it") to the setter in the center-front position. One point is also awarded to the team that wins the rally. Additional points are earned by completing the play over the net—one point for a two-contact play and two points for a three-contact play. No points are awarded if the team doesn't receive the ball and pass it to the center-front position. Alternate serves between teams, regardless of which team wins the rally. Rotate players after each rally.

Variations

To make the game easier for younger or less skilled players, do any of the following:

- Have a coach serve or a player toss easy balls directly to the receiver.
- Allow servers to start closer to the net.
- Award one point for receiving the serve and passing to any position, and award three points for receiving the serve and passing the ball to the center-front position ("nailed it").
- Play 3v4 and rotate a player to the receiving side after each rally.

To make the game more challenging for older or more skilled players, do any of the following:

- Award points only after three consecutive serves have been received and passed to the center-front position ("nailed it").
- Make the target zone smaller.
- Award points only if the first ball is called by the receiver and passed appropriately.
- Play 3v4 with the setter switching sides of the net (to set for the other team) as the ball goes over.
- Require passers to rotate after the ball goes over the net each time.
- Take away a point for not passing a ball that can be kept in play.
- Have passers try to get three points in a row (passers get one point for nailed passes and one point for missed serves) before servers get three points in a row (servers get one point for an immediate point on the serve—called an *ace*—and one point for passes outside the target area).

Pinball Passes

Goal

To work on forearm passes.

Description

Play 3v3 or 4v4 on a court appropriately sized for the age group of your players. To begin, a player on team A serves the ball to team B. Players have two options for play:

- Option 1: Player 1 (P1) on team B receives the ball and makes a forearm pass to player 2 (P2). P2 then makes a forearm pass to another player (P3), who forearm passes the ball back to P1. P1 then overhead passes the ball over the net back to team A (a total of four passes and four points for team B).
- Option 2: Player 1 (P1) receives the ball and makes a forearm pass to player 2 (P2). P2 makes a forearm pass to another player (P3), who forearm passes the ball back to P1. P1 forearm passes back to P3, who forearm passes to P2, who then forearm passes to P1. P1 then overhead passes the ball over the net back to team A (a total of seven passes and seven points for team B).

When the ball is passed over the net, the other team will go through the same sequence of forearm passes. Play is continuous until the rally ends. Alternate serves between teams, regardless of which team wins the rally. Award an extra point for winning the rally. Rotate players or teams after each rally.

Variations

- To make the game easier for younger or less skilled players, allow teams five attempts to make three successful forearm passes.
- To make the game more challenging for older or more skilled players, award a point only when the ball is successfully passed three consecutive times to a specified player, and award extra points if the final contact over the net is an attack.

Target Passing

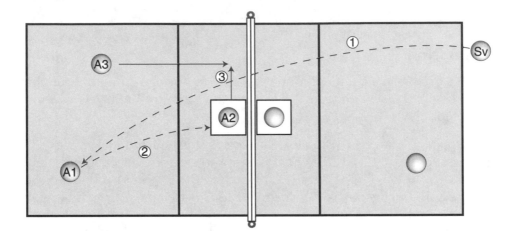

Goal

To forearm pass to the setter position.

Description

Play 3v3 or 4v4 on a court appropriately sized for the age group of your players. To begin, team B serves the ball to team A. Player 1 (A1) receives the ball and makes a forearm pass to player 2 (A2), who is positioned inside a marked five-foot-by-five-foot area in front of the net, as shown in the diagram. A2 sets the ball, and player 3 (A3) hits the ball back over the net. One point is awarded for forearm passes that go into the marked area in front of the net and can be successfully set. Play is continuous until the rally ends. Alternate serves between teams, regardless of which team wins the rally. Rotate players after each rally.

Variations

- To make the game easier for younger or less skilled players, only require the ball to be successfully forearm passed into the target area (without being set) for points; start with the coach serving or a player tossing the ball to initiate the rally; start the server or tosser in close to the net.
- To make the game more challenging for older or more skilled players, play 2v2; decrease the size of the target area to three feet by three feet; move the target area to the right side; or require the second contact to be a forearm (or overhead) pass to a five-foot-by-five-foot hitter's target in the left-front or right-front position.

I Can Pass

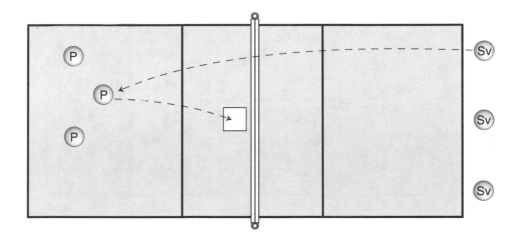

Goal

To improve accuracy of forearm passes.

Description

Play in a court appropriately sized for the age group of your players. Three servers are at the service line on one side of the net; three passers are positioned in the opposite court, with a large garbage can set up in front of the net in the setter's target position, as shown in the diagram. The server serves the ball over the net, and the passers use forearm passes to pass the ball into the garbage can. Two points are awarded each time a ball goes into the can (even if it bounces out). Servers serve five balls each, and then passers and servers are rotated out, and new players are brought in. This drill can be run on both sides of the net at the same time.

Variations

- To make the game easier for younger or less skilled players, have the server toss the ball over the net; allow two contacts to get the ball into the can; move the service area closer to the target can; or use more than one can in the target area.
- To make the game more challenging for older or more skilled players, use smaller target cans; allow the passer who gets the ball into the can to replace the server; or have the server run to the other side of the court to join the passing line, while the passer who received the ball rotates to the serving line.

In the Zone

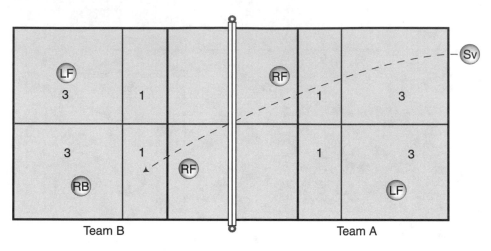

Team B   Team A

Goal

To improve the accuracy of serves.

Description

Play 3v3 on a court appropriately sized for the age group of your players. Each half of the court is divided into four zones. For team A, a server (Sv) is at the service line, and players are in the left- and right-front zones. For team B, players are positioned in the left- and right-back and the right-front zones in the opposite court, as shown in the diagram. The server must serve the ball into one of the four zones. Three points are awarded if the serve goes into one of the two back zones; one point is awarded if the serve goes into one of the two front zones. Two bonus points are awarded if the server first calls the zone she will serve into and the ball goes there. The receiving team in the opposite court should attempt a three-hit (pass, set, attack) sequence and send the ball back over the net. Alternate serving team after each rally. Each server serves three balls before rotating positions.

Variations

- To make the game easier for younger or less skilled players, award points for any service over the net (one point if the ball goes over and out of bounds; two points if the ball goes over and stays in bounds; three points if the ball goes over and into the appropriate zone); move the service area closer to the net; or lower the net.
- To make the game more challenging for older or more skilled players, play 2v2; award points only if the player can call the zone where her serve will go; award points only if the ball touches the ground in the zone called; reduce the size of the zones; or increase the number of zones.

Dig 'Em High

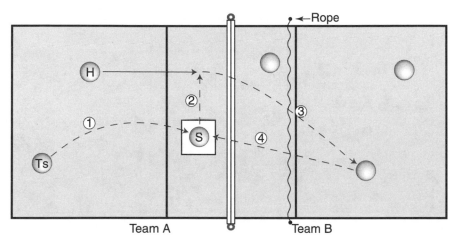

Team A   Team B

Goal

To dig the ball effectively.

Description

Play 3v3 or 4v4 on a court appropriately sized for the age group of your players. A target rope is suspended parallel to the top of the net as high or higher than the net height (attach it to walls or to roll-away standards). This rope is positioned about three meters off the net (approximately at the attack line) as shown in the diagram. Players on team B are in their defensive positions on the court. For team A, players are positioned as a setter and hitters as shown (tape is placed on the floor to mark a starting point for the setters on team A and B). To begin, a player on team A (Ts) tosses or overhead passes the ball to the setter (S), who sets the ball to the third player, the hitter (H). The hitter then attacks the ball over the net. Players on team B must hold their positions until team A's left-front hitter (H) player hits the ball. Players may then move to pursue and dig the ball. The goal is for team B to dig the ball high and over the rope to the center-front setter (S) position—the setter—to score points. Two points are awarded for each dig over the rope directly to the setter's target position; one point is awarded for any dig up and over the rope anywhere along its length.

Variations

- To make the game easier for younger or less skilled players, lower the target rope or award two points for a dig over the rope anywhere along its length, with any dig up high anywhere on the court scoring one point; or increase the size of the passing target and move it deeper into the court.
- To make the game more challenging for older or more skilled players, make the setter's target zone smaller or closer to the net so that it is more difficult to score.

Block-Out

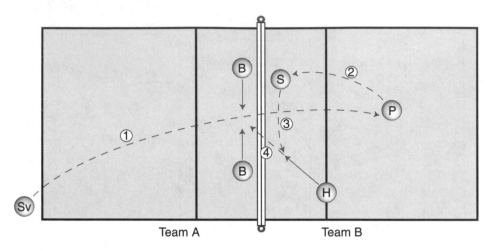

Team A   Team B

Goal

To block attacks effectively.

Description

Play 3v3 on a court appropriately sized for the age group of your players. For team A, two players are positioned at the net (B), and one player is at the service line (Sv). For team B, one player is positioned to receive serve (P), and the other two players are at the net and attack line (S and H). To begin, a player on team A serves or tosses the ball over the net to team B. One player on team B receives the serve and passes to the setter, who sets the ball for the third player to hit. The players at the net for team A prepare to make a block, based on the type of attack executed by team B. Three points are awarded for a successful block that ends the rally; two points are awarded if the block prevents the ball from entering team A's court but the ball is kept in play by team B; one point is awarded for a block in which the ball is touched but kept in play by team A. Play is continuous until the rally ends. Alternate serves between teams, regardless of which team wins the rally. Rotate players after each rally.

Variations

- To make the game easier for younger or less skilled players, lower the net; award points for correct block movement, formation, or balls touched by the blockers; or restrict the blockers to a smaller section of the net where they perform single blocks.
- To make the game more challenging for older or more skilled players, play 4v4 or 5v5; award points only for blocks that end the rally; require all blocks along the net to be double blocks; or add a second (and possibly a third) hitter.

About ASEP

The fourth edition of *Coaching Youth Volleyball* is recommended by USA Volleyball and was written by the American Sport Education Program (ASEP) with volleyball expertise provided by Diana Cole, director of coaching education programs for USA Volleyball, and John Kessel, director of membership development and disabled programs.

USA Volleyball is the national governing body for the sport of volleyball in the United States and is recognized by the Fédération Internationale de Volleyball (FIVB) and the United States Olympic Committee (USOC). Its membership includes more than 200,000 players, coaches, officials, and parents. USA Volleyball's Coaching Accreditation Program (CAP) accepts ASEP's Coaching Youth Volleyball online course as a CAP module equivalent for certification purposes.

ASEP has been developing and delivering coaching education courses since 1981. As the nation's leading coaching education program, ASEP works with national, state, and local sport organizations to develop educational programs for coaches, officials, administrators, and parents. These programs incorporate ASEP's philosophy of "Athletes first, winning second."

BE THE BEST VOLLEYBALL COACH YOU CAN BE, AND COACH WITH CONFIDENCE!

If you've made the commitment to be a youth coach, why not be the best coach you can be?

The American Sport Education Program's Coaching Youth Volleyball online course offers you an easy-to-navigate online class that you can take at your own pace in the comfort of your own home.

Complete with audio, animation, interactive quizzes, downloadable coaching aids, and online test, the course provides you with an engaging, interactive learning experience. From this course, you'll gain field-tested tips on how to run your team, communicate with players, provide basic first aid, plan and conduct practices, and keep it all fun.

You'll receive all of these valuable resources:

- 12-month access to the online course and test
- 12-month access to the "Coaches Clipboard" featuring downloadable reading material, practice plans, checklists, and other coaching aids
- Certificate of completion and three-year ASEP coaching certification
- Entry in the National Coaches Registry, an online listing of certified coaches

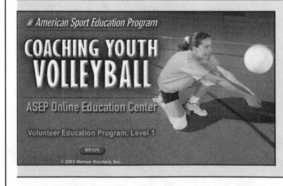

USA Volleyball's Coaching Accreditation Program (CAP) accepts Coaching Youth Volleyball online course as a CAP module equivalent for certification purposes.

Enroll today! Visit www.ASEP.com and select "Course Catalog" from the "Quick Clicks" menu.

A DIVISION OF HUMAN KINETICS

Volume discounts available!
Call 800-747-5698
for more information.

WWW.ASEP.COM

IT'S WORTH IT!

Coaches impact a sport program at every level - athletes, parents, officials, other coaches, the community. Through coaching education, you can help ensure the impact is a positive one.

The American Sport Education Program (ASEP) has been training coaches for more than 25 years. Rooted in the philosophy of "Athletes First, Winning Second," our Volunteer Coaches Education Program is the ideal training ground for coaches of athletes ages 14 and under. Numerous national sport organizations, youth sport organizations, and park and recreation agencies have partnered with ASEP to educate their coaches, and we can do the same for your organization. Contact ASEP today!

American Sport Education Program
A DIVISION OF HUMAN KINETICS

THE LEADING PROVIDER OF YOUTH, HIGH SCHOOL, AND ELITE-LEVEL SPORT EDUCATION

A S E P

WWW.ASEP.COM • 800-747-5698

About USA Volleyball Coaching Education Programs ... *GET CERTIFIED!*

IMPACT - This 4 Hour introductory coaching course, open to ANY coach, includes a Manual and Certificate of completion. IMPACT certifies attendees to coach in the USAV Junior Club Program, and also counts as the Foundations of Coaching Class requirement toward the USAV Coaching Accreditation Program (CAP) Level I certification.

CAP Level I - This 1.5 day course, open to ALL coaches, includes 10 hours of core CAP instruction plus three elective Modules, textbooks and materials (*Coaching Volleyball: Building a Winning Team,* and supplemental handouts), and follow-up certification test. Certification is valid for 4 years.

CAP Level II - This 2 day course, open to Level I certified coaches, includes 10 hours of core CAP instruction plus four elective Modules, textbooks and materials (*Volleyball Coach's Survival Guide* and Supplemental Handouts), and follow-up certification test. Certification is valid for 4 years.

CAP Level III - This 3-4 day course, open to Level II certified coaches, includes approximately 24 hours of classroom and on-court instruction plus all Modules necessary for certification, textbooks and materials (*Course Notebook, Gender and Communication, USOC Sport Psychology Training Manual, Critical Thinking on Setter Development, Periodization Training for Sports),* follow-up certification test and Outreach Project Evaluation. Certification is valid for 4 years.

VCAP - The 4 hour Volleyball Conditioning Clinics are open to all coaches interested in learning how to condition their athletes without a weight room. VCAP clinics may be used as modules toward re-certification requirements for CAP I, II or III.

USA Volleyball
Education

USA Volleyball
IMPACT Program

Our Goal is YOUR Success!

USA Volleyball
Coaching Accreditation Program

For more information visit www.usavolleyball.org or contact USA Volleyball at 719-228-6800 or CAP@usav.org